Thoughts That Move Energy

ALLOWING - AWARENESS - SUPPORT - APPRECIATION - EMPOWERMENT

JULIE MERRICK

Contents

Introduction

Friend, I am a seeker and an occasional finder. Raised in a religion that claimed to be the only true one, my early path was accepting the answers I'd been given and working to stay in the cage God intended for me. But tight bounds grow tiresome and the freedom to fly was in my future. It wasn't an easy escape. The mental bars held far longer than the physical ones.

One of the first books I read after leaving Mormonism, was *Conversations with God* by Neale Donald Walsch. In it, God says to Neale, "How can I tell you what truth is, if you are convinced you already know?" This sentence burned itself into my mind, shaking loose indoctrination and pushing me to seek questions more than answers. To value curiosity over conviction; inquiry over confidence; mystery over certainty.

Something remarkable is afoot here; that I believe. And no God exists who has an agenda for my life. So many incredible teachers have written about their journeys, insights, and discoveries and I thank them. Their way informed my own. Not by revealing *the* correct path but adding information to the map. That is my intention here - to offer up a field journal for your exploration. To share thoughts I've found that move energy.

When I first felt to write a book, I thought the title would be *The Energy School*. But school is such a loaded word that I changed my mind. Let's say we did come here to learn what it is to be human and how energy works in time and space. Earth would not be a program we needed for any required reason (like earning a degree or soul expansion) but an education we were eager to get. From our position outside the game, I think we viewed it as a two-minute ride so there wasn't much concern over its intensity or the hills that would be hell to climb. A brief foray into reality is what we wanted and here we are.

It is with great freedom I explore energy fields because I can and I want to. At the end of the day, subjective truths are a moving target which adds to their appeal. Try them on. Do they fit? Are they comfortable? Are the colors what you wanted? Are you satisfied or on the hunt for better? The closet of meaning belongs to us. We decide what stays and goes.

Thoughts that Move Energy has come together slowly. My older daughter told me it was too long and she was right. Ten energy fields for one book, was five too many. Allowing, awareness, support, appreciation and empowerment are the energies here. Freedom, worthiness, enthusiasm, ease and connection come next. Friend, it thrills me to move this work from my computer to your hands. I hope it makes the cut for your closet.

<u>The Nature of Reality</u> – before we jump into the first energy field, let's visit my closet of meaning and lay some groundwork. I am drawn to the possibility we are each a Story-self, a Light-self and the Animating Force we could call God - but won't.

The Animating Force is not a person; it is not a being on a throne or a father figure we can pray to; it isn't even the orchestrator of the game. It is a Field of All Possibilities, encompassing all that is and ever will be. Neutral, it has no opinions, no preferences, no desires. The Field makes no decisions and pushes no outcomes. It is the source of all consciousness, but is not conscious. It is the genesis of all creation but creates nothing. It is the repository of all love but is not loving. To be everything simultaneously is to be in a holding state, not an expressing one. That's where we come in – as projections from the Field.

Our Story-self is the singular perception, personal life we are each living. Although we eventually merge this story with our Light, it is mainly experienced within a time/space continuum and has beginning and end points. Game-adjacent – humans are the primary players here.

Our Light, or Inner Being, is far less confined by time and space but still holds a particular identity and personality. A composite of many Story-selves, She exists in a dimension of greater complexity than our own. Understanding this dimension in detail would compromise the game. What helps is understanding that our story is Her creation and She couldn't be more invested in our wellbeing. The personal love we feel emanates from Her.

The creative medium is an organizing force that responds to the focus, will and intention of all projections from the Field. We choose and the medium responds to our choice. Consciousness writes code that the creative medium runs.

The Universe is a catch-all term without a clear definition. The teachings I've studied use it to reference the Field, the Light, the creative medium, reality, and sometimes the entire process. Context usually reveals the meaning intended so boxing it in seems inadvisable.

ONE

The Energy of Allowing

Life needs nothing to occur except that which is occurring.
~ Neale Donald Walsch

Allowing is the first energy I want to explore with you, and not because I think it's the most important one. I don't. Connection holds that distinction. But in a world of extreme contrast, even empowered beings of Light (which I believe we are) have limited maneuverability until we embody acceptance in our human form. The energy of allowing gets top billing because it is the base we build on. Without it, our potential for thriving is thwarted over and over again.

Consider for a moment Maslow's hierarchy of needs and its premise that higher states of development, including self-actualization, are unattainable until survival is secured. If someone is pointing a loaded gun at us or we're starving and food can't be found, we're in crisis mode, and our attention will be directed there. Which makes obvious sense. No one gazes in wonder at the stars while worried they won't be around five minutes from now. Less obvious but equally valid is the assertion that conscious creation has its own bedrock: allowing. We can't effectively summon blissful energies like freedom, enthusiasm, or awareness into our experience until we look long and hard at the problem we have with contrast and learn to soften our resistant energy.

Resistance feels like a shoe rubbing a sore on our foot. Allowing feels like taking the shoe off. One is to carry a heavy box, navigate a frenzied freeway, or struggle to silence a screeching smoke alarm. The other lets us put the box down, exit to a quieter street, and turn off the blasted alarm. Resistance triggers unease. Much like a sensory input disorder where incoming stimuli are too intense and touch, scents, sights, and sounds feel assaulting. Nothing is okay. We can't get comfortable. We can't stop ruminating and we find ourselves drawn to addictive behaviors that offer a break from the turmoil. But know this: in a tug of war with reality, we can put down our end of the rope. We can learn to surrender and, like Life, need nothing to occur except that which is occurring.

How big is the fight going to be?

One day I was born, then everything bothered me.
And that brings us up to date.
~anonymous

This observation strikes me as both humorous and helpful, lessening my resistance to my own resistance. Comrades, we are not alone in being

2

bothered by much of what happens here. In fact, I think it would be odd if we weren't. All manner of undesirable things will make our radar, so the question isn't whether there will be a fight but how **big** is the fight going to be?

When I first began exploring spiritual teachings, a friend (who was a Science of Mind practitioner) recommended getting out of our own way. For years, I believed this advice was like the Taylor Swift lyrics - *It's me, hi, I'm the problem, it's me* - which is a close but not quite accurate assessment. We are not in the way because <u>**we** are a problem</u> but because <u>we **have** a problem</u> – our fight with reality. A battle with two fronts, we're either trying to protect ourselves from contrast or end it altogether.

The energy of allowing does not ask us to eliminate negativity, which is good because I've had little success doing so. Don't look there - because it's unpleasant and should be avoided doesn't work for me. Look where you will, have the reaction you have, but don't make a federal case out of it, does. A smaller fight. At times, I have access to thoughts that chill me out; at other times, I need to be scared, accept it, and watch fear come and go. I need to get mad, accept it, and watch anger come and go. When I kick hard against my negative responses, it's throwing bigger punches and traps me in the ring. Opponents attack from all sides and no bell offers a reprieve. A smaller fight isn't apathy or hopelessness. It's a gentler way of being in this world.

My goal in exploring energy fields is to be enticed. I want to find and feel their essence until I'm convinced I both want and can have them. However, the energy of allowing is unique in that its polarity runs interference all the time. Resistance is like a pothole impeding our progress. When the hole is small, we can walk around it and get where we'd like to go. My personal level of being bothered often covers the entire road, and this must be addressed. I can't withdraw the invitation for so much resistance in my life if I'm unclear on how I'm asking for it in the first place. My hope, then, is that the considerations to come leave us both enamored of allowing and informed about resistance.

A Fault Line

It's quite a thing to inhabit a world like this one. We might enjoy our first few years on planet Earth, toddling around discovering all kinds of fascinating things. But it doesn't take long before the concerns surrounding us begin to register. More likely than not, the adults responsible for our care are struggling, and we start absorbing the message life isn't safe. Our bodies take hits – falling ill or being injured, our budding identities get hobbled by criticism and control, and those whose connection we need most may be checked out and unavailable to us. We find ourselves contending with a collective consciousness so steeped in fearful resistance that survival begins taking precedence over exploration.

I live near a beautiful canyon, and years ago, a truck driver was flung to his death when a strong gust of wind lifted his empty semi-truck over a bridge, crashing him into the rocks below. Such a passing leaves one thinking, *Gads, I guess it was his time to go!* But whose existence isn't precarious? This reality sits on a fault line and of course, it's alarming. How could it be otherwise? At any moment, fortune may favor or destroy us and although we play an integral part here, I'm certain our Story-selves are not calling all the shots. This time and space adventure is a mirage and illusions are untenable, beginning to fade the moment they arise. We are on our way out from the second we arrive here. Grasping at shadows is pointless, and the possibility of spending a lifetime striving to secure what slips away not at all far-fetched. The bottom line is we can't save ourselves in an illusion, but we can <u>embrace our choice to exist in one</u>.

When we fully accept the unstable nature of this world, it becomes possible to live wholeheartedly - not because we've secured safety for our story, but because we've made peace with its absence.

Grounded

Our family played a virtual reality game my high-tech son and daughter-in-law purchased during the Christmas holiday. The Last Guardian Demo was so intense I pressed my leg against the couch to stay grounded during my turn. My visual senses reported I was crossing a precarious ledge. The pressure reminded me I was safe in my living room.

When I consider the possibility this human undertaking could be a game, real and not real at the same time, I'm receptive to the energy of allowing. Obstacles strike me more as interesting components than reasons to be terrified or ticked off, and the contrast in this human simulation seems less of a drawback and more of a selling point. We may have paid top dollar to be here. There's a bit of irony in playing a rudimentary virtual reality game from within what could be one of the most incredible virtual realities ever. Humans playing games within a game, and none the wiser!

I don't just find this speculation interesting; I find it meaningful. What if there were no set-in-stone rules for processing what is happening here? If our choices were vast and varied? A pertinent question to ask is *how taken in do I want to be*? I choose to believe I want this crazy ride or I wouldn't be on it and that I have options here. Summoning the essence of my actual home into this temporary one means I can explore with more elation and less trepidation. Getting grounded is my prerogative and is in no way cheating the game.

How do we phone home in the middle of such a fantastical departure and keep our leg pressed against the couch? I think we're surrounded by clues - hints that more is happening here than we realize. My choice to explore energy fields is a beacon I've been following for a long time. When I tune into nature with **awareness,** a world of magic arises that's a dead giveaway. When I have a go at mindfulness with **peace,** a calm descends upon me not of this world. When I create with **enthusiasm,** direct my thoughts with **empowerment**, or approach other beings with **connection**, reality shape-shifts before me. When I **allow** contrast - the mold cracks, exposing a home I never left. I'm still crossing a distressing human ledge, but no longer so paralyzed by fear I want to end my turn.

Just Here for the Popcorn

Do you remember Judith Viorst's children's book *Alexander and the Horrible, Terrible, No Good Very Bad Day?* Where some days are like that, even in Australia? Life happens. Much of it good, some of it not. When frustration and discouragement arise (because the vision for what I want seems miles apart from what is), I'll catch myself eyeing Australia, convinced a fantasy holds better. *Come back to now,* my Light advises me and *take it down a notch*. When I'm working on this book, She recommends taking it down ten notches. Setting the bar high (for our story and its endeavors) seems an admirable intention, but it can be more resistant than allowing.

There is a trick I use when my story feels heavy that never fails to lighten the load. Here's how it works: I announce my reason for existing is simple: I'm just here for the popcorn. That's why I was born. A couple of times a week, I pull out my vintage popper, pour in some oil and a cup of kernels, savor the aroma and watch them explode. After adding plenty of butter and salt, I sit down and enjoy a delicious snack. I'm just here for the popcorn and things could not be going better for me. Can you sense my relief as the shackles fall off my ankles and I walk to freedom? Reject all grandiose possibilities and consider maybe we are here to ride bikes in the shade of trees, provide a comfy home for our cat, or make peanut butter cookies with our grandchildren. It could be our only intention was to plant red tulips, read gothic novels, or relish tortilla chips and spicy salsa. Perhaps we wanted to go fishing, take afternoon naps, or acquire a collection of pink nail polishes. Maybe we heard about the ocean and came to put our feet in the water!

How serious can our stories be if they're ultimately illusions? We set these ridiculously high standards and then don't even enjoy the popcorn. I didn't come here to write a book - that is way too ambitious a reason. I'm not here to create something remarkable. I'm here because the Light I am is already remarkable and She wanted to be a person. This is not to say we can't climb mountains if we want to, but our stories are successful without exception because we're not being asked to conquer but explore, and there's no way to do that wrong.

The Beauty of Storms

I don't just wish you rain, beloved - I wish you the beauty of storms.
~ John Geddes

None of us want a story that hurts but all stories hurt at times. Pain is par for the course here. The energy of allowing does not eradicate distress but transforms it into something with which we can create. Not that we must adopt some *bring on the rain* philosophy (although who's to say this couldn't be an empowering way to live?), but calmly accept storms happen here.

A story without contrast would be boring and offer little of value. No one is really interested in such a narrative, yet don't we all walk around disgruntled because we suppose that is precisely what we want and don't have (and imagine someone else does)? Complicated stories are the only kind which exist, and for good reason, they make us more. When I express a desire to live in greater love and less fear, I'm not attempting to rid myself of contrast but make peace with it. Challenges add depth to the captivating lives we're living.

I am intrigued by the idea of embracing rain and how that choice could bolster the energy of allowing. The above quote by John Geddes moves me to take in the full spectrum of what it is to be human. When I imagine Life calling me beloved and wishing me the beauty of storms, my anger becomes acceptance; my weakness, courage; my pain, love. Barriers keeping the Light from warming me dissolve, and the gap between who I imagine I am and who I genuinely am, shortens.

Henry Wadsworth Longfellow once said the best thing one can do when it is raining is let it rain. This is the energy of allowing - <u>letting the rain fall</u>. Can I accept what happens and give consent to my own story? Can I find the beauty in storms?

Sweet Pickles

The non-physical entity called Abraham teaches the art of allowing. Reality is compared to a dinner buffet where we serve ourselves and we're encouraged to select the entrees we want and not concern ourselves with those we don't. Let's explore this analogy a bit. Imagine I'm in this buffet line, picking and choosing what I want, when I glance down and on my plate is a serving of sweet pickles. What the hell?! I hate sweet pickles, they're the worst. I find it hard to believe anyone enjoys these nasty little gherkins. I must have unknowingly dished them up but I do not want them so into the garbage they go. But when I sit down at the table to eat, there they are, back on my plate. What the heck is going on?

What's going on is this: reality is serving me a dish I do not want and I'm going to have to eat it. (The pushing sensation you may feel after reading that sentence is resistance.) Wait a minute, can't we withdraw our attention from the sweet pickles and they'll go away? Maybe. But in my experience, my willingness to eat the pickles (not like them, eat them) is the one choice that consistently sets me free. Evidence Exhibit A: a friend of mine was born with type one Diabetes, an entree that would be to no one's liking. Accepting her condition isn't going to make it go away. She can't chuck it

9

into the trash and be done with it. It's a limitation she has to eat and it's only a problem if she can't make peace with it. Allowing is accepting the parameters. Resistance is fighting them.

I do suspect we have the underlying ability to heal ourselves from any disease and transcend all limitations here because they are illusions. Like Neo in *The Matrix*, we could wake up and suspend the bullets. Unlike Neo, we chose this dream and this incredible human experience and I do not believe we walked through the entrance just to find the exit. When we accept whatever reality is serving, we're okay with dinner. Maybe tomorrow a new dish will be available (perhaps dill pickles, which I like,) but maybe not.

When I first learned about the Law of Attraction, I found it cut and dried which was comforting because it offered the possibility of control. But it never panned out like I expected. Please explain to me how my friend with diabetes focused her way into her disease and I'll respond it isn't simple. Reality does a number on us. No one jumps into this pool and stays dry. We're in the water, doing our best to swim. At times non-physical teachers come across flippant to me. Lacking in compassion, I wonder if they've ever been in the pool. I've known for a long time I wanted to teach from within the game, applying every insight to my on-the-ground, in-the-room-where-it's-happening perspective.

To Open or Close?

Suffering is rampant in this world because resistance is rampant in this world. We're troubled over things that happened to us in the past, both real and imagined. We're worried over things that might happen to us in the future. We're bothered by opinions that differ from ours, agitated by situations we have no control over and shaken by stories of injustice which happened long before we were born. We're dismayed about things happening in countries we'll never visit, to people we'll never know. One person will take on all manner of problems throughout time and then struggle with a rational longing to escape this nightmare.

The separating fog necessary to exist here (and so buy into the illusion) means the bad stuff frequently causes us to believe the game has malfunctioned and then to erroneously suppose our resistant energy will rectify matters. Ignorant of the hows and whys, we struggle. But there is no glitch.

We are not small, easy targets trying to survive in a huge, harsh world but indestructible Beings of Light, creating in a biological dream world. A dream world that is downright intense. Allowing is an opening energy that reveals more of who we truly are; resistance is a closing energy that shuts this knowledge down. The choice to open rather than close is the solution we're seeking, no matter how exposing it seems. The Light comes to and through us when we accept whatever arises, including any impulse to fight.

Road Report: (how this information is playing out for me right now) A conservative radio personality recently passed away, and I'd forgotten how much I disliked this man. He made a large amount of money being a bottom feeder - exploiting fear, prejudice, and the meanest impulses those energies bring about. I told my husband I wondered what kind of personalized hell-loop this guy found himself in (a reference fellow fans of the show *Lucifer* will get.) But this is me, buying into the misguided assumption that resistance will undermine and bring down the kind of evil this man incarnated. (Evil being fractionalization from the whole.) If this worked, a certain news station would have been off the air ages ago. But it doesn't work. To open is not to look at the energy of disconnection manifesting here and call it good. It isn't good, but it is not a mistake. We are where we are in the process of evolving into Light. What I feel when I open is compassion - not approval. Upon his death, this man returned to the extraordinary Light he always was but couldn't yet personify. When I close in resistance, I'm not embodying my Light either, as my harsh judgments indicate. When we allow, the Light reveals all stories' worthiness, no matter how they are playing out.

The second example is more trivial. Waking up in the middle of the night and being unable to go back to sleep is of concern. After completing a masterclass course on the importance of sleep, I'm paranoid about getting enough rest. The stats on the early death rates of people who routinely sleep five hours or less a night scare me, which is not even my situation. I can't relax and go back to sleep because I'm so upset about not being able to relax and go back to sleep. Can I open to this unwanted situation, and what happens if I do?

What happened was a profound shift. The instant I became entirely willing to feel my anxiety and not push it away, it disappeared. So much so I questioned if it had been there at all. My closed thoughts of *dammit, not again!* became open thoughts of *this sucks - oh well*. Weeks have passed and I'm still waking up, but the hyper-alert thing isn't happening as often. I feel guided to turn my attention toward any dream details I can remember in a soft, nondescript way. Calm, I slip right back into slumber and this pleases me. Do I expect this problem is gone for good? I have no idea and it doesn't matter. Allowing doesn't mean we stop wanting what we want. It means we stop attempting to manipulate situations through resistance.

When we see first-hand how refusing to accept reality never serves us, it becomes a hundred times easier to let things go. But this positive outcome brings up an issue of its own.

Really Letting Go

Letting go to get what you want is not really letting go.

I came across an article on this topic written by a man who shared his frustration that the heat in his apartment wasn't working and the elevators were sporadic. He wanted better and who would blame him? While venting in a phone call to his mother, he decided to stop complaining and put his spiritual beliefs into practice. Accepting the unwanted conditions, he put on a sweater, wrapped up in a blanket, and took the stairs when necessary. Soon after, the heat kicked on and the elevators began working.

I found myself thinking about my sewing business and a large pile of repaired clothing that had been sitting on my shelf for four months. Repeated phone calls were not being returned and I had decided to let it go, thinking this would result in a resolution. After reading this blog, however, it struck me I hadn't *really let go* because my underlying intention was to push the outcome I wanted.

When we choose to live in allowance and place no demands on reality, circumstances improve dramatically. That the man's heat and elevators began working, did not surprise me. When we let things be what they are, we tend to get what we want. Knowing this is problematic, however, as it may lure us to seek control from a covert position. <u>Really letting go</u> is like flipping a switch and enabling a current of acceptance. The energy of manipulation shorts that circuit without exception. We must reach for the place within us that needs nothing to change to be at peace. As for my work situation? I flipped the switch, accepted whatever might happen, and promptly forgot all about it. The following afternoon a call came in from this customer (it did not immediately dawn on me who she was!) She apologized, explaining she had been out of the country, and promised to pick up her items the next day. I find myself searching for an example where I've accepted what is and things didn't work out and nothing comes to mind. The craziest element here is acceptance means things DO work out – no matter what happens. There have been times when I didn't get paid for my work, which wasn't something I wanted. The energy of allowing means I can't find a problem there.

How can we know when we've *really let go*? All tension leaves our bodies. Our thoughts are no longer obsessively drawn to our concern and we can easily put our attention elsewhere. We aren't hindered by our preferences or using them as a reason to fight. What seemed a huge deal isn't anymore and we'd be hard-pressed to explain why we were so concerned in the first place.

Am I in pain or am I suffering?

Some people awaken spiritually without ever coming into contact with any meditation technique or any spiritual teaching. They may awaken simply because they can't stand the suffering anymore.
~ Eckhart Tolle

The awakening stories of Eckhart Tolle and Byron Katie are fascinating. Both spiritual teachers underwent intense suffering, followed by a profound shift in their perception. The acceptance they now embody leaves me longing for a similar unfolding. Wouldn't it be nice to rip the band-aid off and be done with it? To wake up instantly and remember we are Love and all is well? However, this particular path doesn't seem to be a common one. Taken in by the illusion daily, I struggle to connect with Life because I'm too busy having a problem with it. I buy into this tale to the Nth degree, pushing against things not to my liking and suffer as a result. My fight with reality is exposed by answering this question: *Am I in pain or am I suffering?*

It blows my mind a bit that as an eighteen-year-old, I took a psychology class in college addressing this very issue. My professor shared his research into how resistance affected our perception of physical pain and proposed discomfort is significantly magnified by the mental aversion ordinarily engaged when harm arises. For example, if you hit your finger with a hammer, you will tense up and immediately fight what is happening. Your whole body is thrown into a defensive response and this intensifies pain. After training himself to allow discomfort by focusing on the sensation minus the resistance, he could put a long needle through his arm (I kid you not - in one side and out the other) without flinching. Witnessing this was riveting and his theory helped me better manage dentist visits and labor pains.

We can consciously choose to lessen our suffering by experimenting with this hypothesis. What happens when we focus on a sensation minus the resistance? Curiosity is a good driver here. The next time you're in physical discomfort, deliberately move toward the experience instead of backing away. Stop wanting it gone and observe how it feels. Note the difference in intensity. See for yourself how resistance amplifies discomfort. Hurt in our bodies is unambiguous (and typically passes) so analyzing a move from resisting to allowing is less complicated than it is with emotional distress. But emotional pain is where we often get stuck and suffer on a loop.

Change is constant in a biological world as time marches on, but do you ever feel like you've been on the same emotional ride forever? The reason for this is straightforward - we've stopped the game. It's helpful to understand experience transforms upon completion. Think of it like the board game, Jumanji, where one turn must be completed before moving on to the next. Reality will not let us jump ahead and skip a turn. A troubling event happens in our story. Resistance and its consort, suffering, show up and cause us to hit the brakes. Everything comes to a screeching halt because (understandably) we wish to avoid pain. The game wants to continue but can't until we finish the turn. And now we find ourselves in a loop, for reality will keep presenting us with scenarios to complete the round and move on. The scenery, the characters and the details may change, the energy doesn't. It's stuck because we aren't willing to have the human experience we are having. *Am I in pain or am I suffering?* is meant to raise awareness as the only way out is through.

Release the brakes by allowing your own resistance and move into the pain your Light is more than capable of feeling. My belief in the Law of Attraction interferes at times with my ability to allow. Because instead of accepting what is, I seek to change it. Removing what I don't want is the objective. An all-in willingness to play the game gives us power here and points to a paradoxical truth: nothing changes until we fully accept it not changing.

Rubber-band Problems

What we resist, persists. Damn if that isn't hard to believe at times. It seems like we ought to be able to go head-to-head with adversity and bring it down through the power of our will. To force reality to bend the knee and submit to our wishes or push our self to step up and change things for the better.

My husband and I were bored one January and thought we might listen to some encouraging podcasts. A bit of searching around uncovered programs with this frenzied, personal coaching, self-improvement, over-the-top energy. Yuck. Even the saner/softer shows carried an underlying 'how to fix your life!' tone. I hope this book does not come across this way - but leaves you (a worthy, empowered being) encouraged over your energetic options here.

All the *choose your hard, build self-trust, be a winner* hype rubs me wrong. So much resisting, so little allowing. What we have are rubber band problems where we push and pull, stretching to create as much distance as possible between ourselves and our issues. Tension builds and it becomes harder and harder to keep what we don't want at bay. Rubber bands only stretch so far before they come back and come back hard.

Case in point - the battle of the bulge. I followed an effective low-carb diet for a number of years. It wasn't *no fruit* extremism yet still pretty restrictive. The upside - I quit overeating (no one binges on eggs) and food cravings went away. The downside - it was a hard-to-stick-with, joy suck. I swear one morning I woke up and my body said, *We're not doing this anymore.* And that was that. I'd stretched the rubber band and it snapped back.

An online hypnotist shared subconscious beliefs that keep us from losing weight: *It won't work* (failed previously.) *It isn't worth it* (way too unpleasant.) *If it does work, I'll just gain it back* (as before.) One comment mirrored my own reaction to these observations: I'm pretty sure these thoughts are front and center - not hidden in my subconscious. I wish I was gearing up to give you an easy solution (to the battle of the bulge) but I don't have one. My goal is to snip the band and keep the fight small. To accept I will be tempted to jump back into this fray (and strong arm my body into compliance) and if that happens, it happens. This hard thing is on my plate because our food options are lifeless (driving us to overeat) and we aren't at peace with our bodies. It's complicated and I am not going to demand it be otherwise.

Before I move on to a more encouraging approach, I want to circle back around to the whole make a commitment to yourself and keep it directive. Let's pull back the curtain and expose this idea for the steaming pile of dung it is. Resistance means we will stretch the band and eventually fall off the wagon. It's bad enough our efforts come to naught but now we must declare ourselves untrustworthy? (Here's your forehead L stamp because only a loser can't even keep a promise to themselves!) Great energy, no? Imagine, instead, a stamp saying NOT TRUE and firmly ink it onto any idea claiming you aren't enough. Resistance is one big whack-a-mole game – where each knock down leads to a pop up in another spot. Put the mallet down for there is another way.

Allowing asks us to paint with a broad-brush, not zero in on details to alter but accept the whole of it. Whatever **it** is. *In this moment, here I am. This is what I think is happening and the meaning I'm assigning. Here's how I feel about it.* **Accept. Accept. Accept.** (Not believe, accept.) That's how you clip the rubber band. Allow what is happening first, then shift your beliefs or change up your approach if you feel to.

While visiting a record store in Boise, a sales clerk directed me to the back counter. "Restroom key?" I asked as I approached the plexiglass wall. Offended, the man I'd spoken to responded with "I think you're forgetting some word starting with a P?" Wow, I had not meant to be rude and apologized. When I returned the key, he was as friendly as I was upset. I felt like he'd called me out as a Karen (and was horrified I'd behaved like one) and an hour later I was still out of sorts, mentally scrambling to undo what had happened. Trying to change our take on a situation in order to feel better doesn't always work and Life was showing me this. Certainly, our perceptions are questionable and open to new interpretations but that was not the solution here. I needed to allow *where I was, what I thought had happened and how I felt about it.* Accept. Accept. Accept. In the past, an interaction like this one would have distressed me permanently. The energy of allowing set me free in a way no rewrite or rewind could. All desire to change what happened dissolved and I was able to move on.

Love our way into better things

Merging the energies of acceptance and appreciation lets us to love our way into better things, as it disconnects **want** from **need**.

Some Law of Attraction teachings claim if we tell the Universe we **want** something, **want** is what will be reflected. My experience challenges this. Creative pretense is disingenuous. If I'm driving to a job I don't like, while telling the Universe how grateful I am to have a job I love – integrity is missing. The argument is the creative medium (or Universe) can't discern imagination from actuality <u>but I certainly can</u>. Which is why I don't believe starting from an endpoint for manifestation works well. The bullshit isn't fooling me, so there will be resistance on my end. It's trickery that isn't effective and more importantly, isn't necessary.

Wanting is a good thing when we embrace it without **need**. I want ice for the polar bears, citizenship for my immigrant neighbors, policemen who serve and protect us, a government that puts the good of its people first. I want industry that isn't exploitive, connection that eradicates servitude, and non-profit health care that actually is. I want a positive outcome for my husband's back surgery, for the Sacramento Kings to keep winning, to finish this book before I die. Each thing I want is birthed in part from what I don't want but I will never be a summoning force until I clip rubber-band energy - until I free myself from neediness. I do so with one sentence, one caveat, one qualifier – *I'm okay with what happens.* And if I <u>can't</u> say this and truly mean it then I go to sentence number two, which also clips the band: *I'm **not** okay with what happens and I accept this.* The second thought is more powerful than you might think, creating an opening for our Light to come in and make up the difference, which She can and will. Peace always follows acceptance.

So, drive to the job you don't like while telling the Universe the kind of job you'd love to have. Maybe it pays better, with engaging work and likeable co-workers. Maybe you want ample time off and a sense of belonging. It could offer a courtyard for breaks, welcome creative input or require no commute. Go for the big fish and think of it as a catch and release endeavor. Reel it in, appreciate the wonder of it, then unhook it and watch it swim away. **Want** without **need.** When I secured a space for my alterations shop in Ketchum it was all I'd wanted and more. An architect had custom-built an entire wall unit with drawers, cupboards and counter space. There were two sunny windows, one with a gorgeous mountain view. There were no stairs, which is rare in a ski town, but ideal for many of my customers. The location was right on main street and yet the rent was affordable. This happened long before I'd thought much about rubber-band energy but looking back I can see how it was a want with little need. I was prepared to make the best of things and the best of things showed up.

Love what you love and then let go. Our best friend and fur kid, Bentley, crossed the rainbow bridge about a year ago, and come spring I want a new corgi. An energetic, ridiculously smart, tri-colored fluff ball with attitude. I want to find an amazing breeder, who's done all the genetic testing, provided early socialization and will agree to not docking his tail. I want our cat, Morty, to fall in love with the new little guy and for them to be the best of friends. I want to find a second family to care for him while I shop each week, so he'll have a happy place to stay should we travel without him. I love each one of these things I want yet *I'm okay with what happens*. I don't make this choice so only joy will bound into my experience but to free myself from neediness and love my way into better things.

Breaking the Spell

The SPELL can be broken just by asking yourself, is what I'm believing true?
~ Byron Katie

In her book *Loving What Is*, Byron Katie presents a questioning process she calls The Work. Inquiry exposes the illusion and leads to acceptance because truth in a fantasy is relative. We're making it all up. We continuously project meaning onto nothing and react accordingly. That's what we do. The Work brings this to our attention and offers relief through a shift in perception.

When I first encountered The Work, I didn't get it. Say I'm in a car accident, or someone lies to me, or my dog passes away, and I'm upset because these things happened. How could such situations and my response to them be untrue? Questioning them seemed illogical. Eventually, I realized this process is not about what is factual or logical in the story. It is the understanding I hold of the story itself. The answers to the questions come from my Light, who is unharmed and at peace. When a thought hurts and I question what is true, She responds from Her perspective.

The premise of Byron's teachings align with *A Course in Miracles*, which teaches: Nothing real can be threatened. Nothing unreal exists. Herein lies the peace of God. We are living these incredible stories that aren't real. What **is** real? Love and Life, for they can't be threatened. The Animating Force (or Life) will never cease to be, and it holds us in an expression (a Story) that will cease to be. One is real; the other is not. I'm not suggesting our stories have no meaning or significance. They do. But they are fleeting expressions of Life, not Life itself, and this distinction offers peace. I'm not seeking to quash my story but lessen the death grip of my unquestioned projections.

These favorite teachings by Byron Katie, offer insight into the energy of allowing:

The only time we suffer is when we believe a thought that argues with what is. How can we know something should have happened? It did. How can we know it is not true? It causes us to suffer.

Without your story, you're perfectly fine. When I set aside concern over the past and future, most of my narrative goes with it and *fine* is what remains.

Forgiveness is discovering that what you thought happened, didn't. It is a tall order to question our story until we realize what we thought happened to us, didn't. The amount of healing which rushes in when we touch down, however briefly, upon this truth is profound. Transformative, the Love which cannot be threatened continually offers us this gift. Not to exit our stories but bring our Light into the mix.

Welcome to the movie of who you think you are. Pass the popcorn. When I break the SPELL of rigid beliefs, it's a better show and I do enjoy popcorn.

A Call to Arms (at the level of cause)

I'm going to go out on a limb here and assume many of you (my friends who are also drawn to the Law of Attraction) have experienced backlash for your positive thinking beliefs. That you've been characterized as naïve and uncaring, villainized as one more interested in seeking your own happiness than promoting justice in the world. (My take on this may be a little harsh.)

Part of me wants to tell the naysayers to fork off already. I'm not giving weight to their opinion about what I believe and how I live. Another part of me (the pondering one) questions if my positions are sound or wishful thinking? Is my belief that rage will never invite peace misguided? Maybe we should fiercely battle the dark side – but maybe not. Yesterday, I cried watching the Iranian soccer team stoically refuse to sing their national anthem during their opening game at the men's World Cup. A woman in the audience was crying as well. The brutal and oppressive government ruling their country sickens me and these people deserve better. I'm so tired of corruption and it feels to me we all deserve better. Ghandi's teaching that an eye for an eye makes the world blind resonates and my experience confirms I can't go seeking out a pound of flesh, determined to destroy those who've harmed others without becoming a drawing force to the energies I do not want. This is not meant to criticize the Iranian revolution but rather question how we approach change.

This topic is going to show up in most of the energy fields I explore. Because I think it's a misconception tripping us up. We get angry about what is and fight against it and little changes. We keep applying the same tactical procedures, push forward an inch and then find ourselves getting pushed right back. Because the energy hasn't shifted. We aren't beckoning what we want but pushing against what we don't. Full-on rubber banding! I'm not interested in quashing men (although watching a video of an Iranian leader saying women are no better than animals, created by God to serve men) it's tempting (as apparently, they don't value women or animals.) What I do want is for men to get their knuckles off the ground and you know what? There is evidence everywhere evolved men exist. Everywhere. I think about my grandsons whom I love so much and I don't want them to be beaten down as a punishment for testosterone poisoning, to feel guilty about being male. Culture and biology make it hard for all of us. What we want does exist and we can put our attention there.

We can let what's happening upset us and then retreat to higher ground. Not because the situation is agreeable or because action is uncalled for but because we know *the energy of alignment with what we want is the most powerful weapon in our arsenal.* That's the arrow we want to shoot because it will hit its target without fail. It will change reality at the level of cause.

I share these thoughts with you because I believe we (believers in the Law of Attraction) have a critical role to play in the advancement of humankind. As we encourage and fortify our position, we become the change we want to see in the world. Do not be deterred by criticism (or seek to change anyone's mind) but stand firm on the base of allowing and build from there. Proclaim there is no hill you are willing to die on (as the world won't benefit long run from another dead person on a hill), but a garden you will tend. What we want needs a place to take root and grow and the vision of Empowered Beings of Light creates this. May we take up arms together at the level of cause, fearlessly wanting without need, and steadfastly summon the dawning of a kinder day.

Flow without Friction

As I bring this section to a close, a vision of a less needy existence has jumped into my imagination and latched on tightly. This is not some pie-in-the-sky fantasy that can never happen. It's a possibility sitting right in front of me waiting to see if I'll choose it. An invitation, not a summons, it feels like I've opened an acceptance letter to The Hogwarts School of Witchcraft and Wizardry, and I'm off to pack my trunk. The energy of allowing is not affirming something you doubt or demanding improvement. It is the unequivocal acceptance of what shows up. It is direct knowledge of the strength in surrender and the absolute certainty nothing is truly amiss.

I believe my Inner Being intended to navigate this story as a story, not leave the stage to reveal a dramatic flight of fancy. We are novels come to life and we can't jump out of the pages of our book without ending the saga. But we don't want to be completely lost in those pages either, for such a book is a tough read. When I allow Life to flow through me without friction, love holds me and I have fewer needs. The contrast hasn't dried up and gone away, but it's no longer the chopping block it was before. My Light is more than capable of thriving here, no matter what I have to eat. If I let her, she will absorb the pain, close the loops, and walk with me into the next turn.

TWO

The Energy of Awareness

At times, my daily routine both bores and irritates me. I look around and think I'm sick to death of sewing, cleaning, cooking, and shopping. There are no movies I want to see, books I feel like reading, or places I'm eager to visit. A sad lack of engagement plagues me, and Hamlet's observation about the world and its uses being stale, weary, and unprofitable hits too close to home.

Charles Kingsley's observation that *"We act as though comfort and luxury were the chief requirements of life when all that we need to make us really happy is something to be enthusiastic about"* appeared to offer a solution. Put into practice, however, it was not consistently helpful. And even gardening could not lift my ennui. It wasn't until I began exploring the energy of awareness and what it creates that I uncovered the root of my discomfort. I feel depleted and uninspired when I've walked off the path of present-moment focus and am perceiving this world through the limited faculties of mind. Stale, weary, and unprofitable is the nature of that viewpoint, as it keeps a lid on wonder and awe. Chasing enthusiasm may help, but (without awareness) can be an escape route to a dead end.

Where I want to go next is the opposite of a dead end. Awareness is a passage into a vista of wonderment. Think Rally. Refresh. Rejuvenate. Think exhilarate. Elevate. Engage. Think of an energy capable of breathing new life into your world. For when we bring our full focus to the present moment more consistently, awareness expands our limited perceptions and leaves us astounded at what we find.

Enchantment

What does the energy of awareness feel like? When I ask myself this question, the recollection of Harry Potter entering a magical tent at the World Cup Quidditch Tournament in the 4th movie comes to mind. Their shelter appears small from the outside, but a spacious, multi-room dwelling greets Harry as he pulls back the canvas door and crosses the threshold. Looking around in awe, he smiles, shakes his head, and slowly tells himself *I love magic*. Awareness feels like that. It is the realization you aren't a muggle in a hum-drum world but a wizard in a mesmerizing one. It is the discovery of enchantment where you thought there was none.

Awareness is the tolling of bells on Christmas Eve, the silence of falling snow, the roar of a jet as it crosses the sky. Music in a minor key, a hidden cove, the twilight hour. The flavor of garden-grown tomatoes, ripe plums, and warm bread. The crackle of burning twigs and a rising wisp of smoke. Awareness feels like huckleberry bushes heavy with fruit, groundhogs sunning themselves in springtime, or a hawk poised for flight. It is the laughter of children, the crunch of gravel beneath tires, the warmth of turned soil.

A collusion of creation, this energy wields the power to sweep us into a reality so enticing words cannot do it justice.

The Right Now in a Big Way

A useful definition for the energy of awareness is to <u>feel the right now in a big way.</u> Two necessary components. The right now by itself won't cut it. And a big way (which is key here) can only happen in the now. Labeling this energy awareness instead of mindfulness was a deliberate choice (even though the terms are often interchangeable) because awareness is neither mind-centered or mind-generated. Our minds aren't bad things, they're small things. While they are fully capable of processing a present moment (which is beneficial), they cannot do so in a big way.

When we process reality through our limited minds, we live unsatisfied. We chase after fantasies we wrongly believe will fill the empty space – the space where our Light should be shining like nobody's business but isn't. We continually dim our essence (as we don't know how not to) and then stumble around in the dark longing for something, anything to make us whole. Friend, I want to share with you one of the most important things I've discovered in all my years of seeking and it is this: **the Animating Force that is our Life, that is our Light, is a processing system.** One humans mostly shut down. Learning to make this system operational changes everything and awareness serves as a litmus test revealing how we're functioning.

My intentions for this section then are twofold: to offer a convincing sales pitch (as to why we want this energy) and to lay out potent ideas (as to how we can get this energy) that leave us both inspired and encouraged.

I feel compelled to promise you that <u>feeling the right now in a big way</u> is worth any price we have to pay and that price is a radical, but achievable, shifting of perception.

Making Good

I'm going to jump in here and sum up what's coming next. Because I don't want you to read any further hoping I'll make good on my promise. I've read books where I felt the teacher was gearing up to offer me something of significance, only to be disappointed when it didn't happen. I know they meant well but the progression from inspiration to application is daunting. It's easy for me to tell you awareness is worth any price we have to pay and much harder to explain why this is so, what it costs and how to pay it. So even if it means repeating myself (as I will delve into these ideas going forward), here are the *why, what,* and *how* I consider most consequential for the energy of awareness.

WHY – When we funnel our consciousness through our human mind it is like surviving on freeze-dried rations when there is an unlimited supply of fresh food available to us. And this poor comparison doesn't begin to reveal the reduction we're talking about here. I'm pretty certain you aren't a newbie to this idea. Like me, you know you have an energy body and are capable of feeling it. But also like me, I suspect a huge portion of your Light is an untapped resource in your human experience. To be blind and then see is a tectonic shift - altering our every perception of what it is to be embodied here.

WHAT – The cost is straightforward. We must transcend the unconscious collective belief as to who we are. We have to step out of the game enough to see we are in a game. We are **not** biological bodies capable of thought. We are **not** souls stuffed into biological bodies capable of thought. We **are** the Light. Now you might be thinking to yourself, *I already know this*. **No, you don't.** If you already knew this you wouldn't be reading this book. You would be outside observing a blade of grass in unspeakable bliss. If I already knew this, I would be outside observing a blade of grass in unspeakable bliss. I'm not trying to be flippant but offering a tool for discernment. Unspeakable bliss is what happens when we know *who* we truly are.

HOW – That's the million-dollar question isn't it? With a make-or-break answer. How do we transcend an unconsciously held collective belief? Particularly one we took on in order to be here. A catch-22, how do we remember we are the Light in a game which requires we forget? The answer is simpler than you might think. But before you get too excited, know this, there is no get-out-of-jail-free card we can draw. Which is okay. The **how** isn't a bypass but a buy-in. Accept the illusion, the forgetting, the limitations, the challenges, the struggles and then turn in the direction of Light. Open to it (in a big way) over and over again, wherever it shows up for you. That is **how** we pay the price. A taste here, a taste there. A connection here, a connection there. A moment here, a moment there. Every pocket of Light is a mirror revealing *who* we are, which leads to bliss. Not some permanent state of euphoria that dissolves reality or erases all pain but a revelatory shift inside the game.

<u>**Road Report:**</u> I'm almost done reading the Pulitzer Prize-winning novel, *Middlesex*, by Jeffrey Eugenides. A gripping story with masterful writing, it's my kind of book. The main character is an intersex man who

narrowly avoids mutilating surgery and hormones to keep him the female he never was. Troubled on his behalf, my mind keeps recycling the injustice of such a hurtful, confusing and complicated situation. Then it turns personal. How can I write about bliss when shit like this happens? Maybe I don't know what I'm talking about and Life is cruel. Wouldn't a loving Universe provide better? Focused small, I'm not at peace with reality.

Where exactly is it, you think you are? Pulled up short, this question reminds me I'm not in a world of ribbons and rainbows, where angels step in and correct all wrongs. This place is high drama, intense experience, and contrast of epic proportions. *Is the Light here?* Yes – and it's showing up for me daily in a family of Swainson's hawks who've nested in a nearby pine tree. All spring and summer I've listened as the fledging screeched for food, watched her grow and marveled as she learned to fly. Besotted, I've observed this brood of three perch beside each other in the early morning hours, taking turns in flight. Not as enamored of me, one adult dived aggressively in my direction and it wasn't a *hello* but a *back the hell off and quit watching us* communication. Predators, I know they can see me far better than I can see them. And now the parents have ditched Hannah (her name in my world). Tough love, for if she's a poor hunter, she'll likely starve to death. More than seventy percent of raptors perish before reaching maturity. Soon these hawks will be migrating as a group to Argentina and I'm hopeful Hannah's parents will come for her. This avian family is a phenomenal Light touching me to my core but their life is no fairy tale. My Story-self takes exception to harsh while my Light reveals the miracle of Hannah is not in her thriving but in her existence. That's the turn, the connection, the focus offering peace and the bliss of exquisite beauty right here, right now.

Waking Up

Most people, even though they don't know it, are asleep. They're born asleep,
they live asleep, they marry in their sleep, they breed children in their sleep,
they die in their sleep without ever waking up. They never understand the
loveliness and the beauty of this thing we call human existence.
~ Anthony De Mello

My oldest brother and his husband are night owls, while my husband and I are morning larks. One recently shared adventure involved leaving our cabin at 9:00 a.m. (a compromise for both couples). As the two of them silently zombied their way up and out the door, we marveled even their Yorkie, Archie, was subdued. The tables turned, however, when late afternoon found the two of us comatose while Shawn cleaned out the car, Robert prepared dinner and Archie bounded after his toys. Seriously, who feels this good at 5:00 p.m.?! Unlike circadian rhythms, living without awareness offers us no alert time, just a blanket of fog no amount of coffee or sleep can lift. Lacking full consciousness, we unwittingly choose a half-life that could be whole.

Laurence Kushner offered this instruction, *"The trick is to pay attention to what is going on around you long enough to behold the miracle without falling asleep. There is another world, right here within this one, whenever we pay attention."* When I keep myself awake long enough to behold the miracle, everything about existence is inexplicably pleasing to me.

A friend once overheard her twelve-year-old son comment to himself (as he swept the kitchen floor) that he wasn't meant for such drudgery. Ah yes, we've all been there. Stuck in a situation not to our liking and feeling put upon. But tedious work and unpleasant circumstances provide ideal conditions for waking up. When a job is arduous or a condition frustrating, the mind wants it over as quickly as possible and our discomfort is palpable. Intentional presence offers immediate feedback and first-hand knowledge of what it is to live an uncomfortable now in a big way. Life is miraculous and when I choose to step into (rather than away from) such happenings, the resulting shift invariably leaves me wondering what the hell just happened?

J.W.N. Sullivan describes it like this, *"It is only in exceptional moods that we realize how wonderful are the commonest experiences of life. It seems to me sometimes that these experiences have an 'inner' side, as well as the outer side we normally perceive. At such moments one suddenly sees everything with new eyes: one feels on the brink of some great revelation. It is as if we caught a glimpse of some incredibly beautiful world that lies silently about us all the time."* The great revelation isn't that we're suddenly pleased to be sweeping the floor but riveted by an encounter with our Light who happens to be sweeping the floor.

Magic Eye Illusions

If you aren't familiar with magic eye illusions (or it's been a long time,) take a minute and check them out. They're interesting and I want to use them as an experiential example of shifting perception. In order to see such illusions, our focus must go from narrowed-in to broadened-out. As we relax our vision, a hidden image gradually rises off the page until it pops. We might see an outline of running horses or a bouquet of flowers. Once this happens, it's fairly easy to continue seeing the image or get it back should it dissolve. Don't stress if you can't do this (certain conditions interfere) as magic eye illusions are cool but not that cool.

A different helpful example is how we can adjust our sensory input to serve a purpose. If someone asks us *what's that noise?* we will turn down seeing and turn up hearing. Or *what's that scent?* we will turn down seeing and turn up smelling. Visual input is dominant but we can easily switch to another sense when we want to. I share these examples because feeling **the right now in a big way** is a conscious adjustment. A choice. A switch. A turn of the dial. I can describe what this movement is like for me which may be helpful to a point. But like a magic eye illusion, firsthand experience is necessary to fully understand it. Unlike a magic eye illusion, the perception of our Light is off-the-charts cool – like *standing-beside-the-ocean* or *on-top-of-a-mountain-connected* kind of cool.

Friend, I'm confident you've felt the right now in a big way or you'd have little interest in this book. But your encounters may have been more of a Light System override (where your part in their happening was negligible) than a purposeful alignment you intended. That was my experience anyway. I had to learn my Story-self was not a small player in this game – but the avatar through which my Light experiences Life here and I could focus in a way that merged both perspectives.

All Systems Go

My spiritual "schooling" was set into motion by contact with teachers (primarily through books) who process their experience through their Light. As I pondered their teachings, a portal began to open and I sensed my energy was much like a light bulb. Permeating every particle of my body, it is most concentrated near my heart yet extends far out from my physical form. If I'm sitting in my office, for example, it travels right through the window and walls. Larger than a ten by twelve-foot room, nothing in this reality obstructs it. This is not to suggest its size needs measuring but more to emphasize the whole of who I am was more significant than I'd realized.

At the same time, I began noticing how my attention was predominantly held in a small area slightly above and in front of my physical eyes. Easiest to discern while doing mentally challenging tasks (like writing), it's where the narrative runs. Both a mind center and a storyboard, whatever held my interest lived there. All sensory input would beeline straight to this point and it wasn't a particularly peaceful place to be. There are some unpleasant truths about my mind center/storyboard. Left to her own devices, she likes to worry - a lot. She judges, ruminates, projects and buys a lot of interesting trouble with her attention. Safety is always priority one and her values reflect this. Frankly, she's a bit of a downer.

On the upside, as I began giving more attention to my Light, strange things began happening. My mind center/storyboard didn't power off but the origin of its' perceptions shifted. My Light has different priorities and this was pivotal. Fear was the first thing to go and was replaced with exhilaration and contentment. Time seemed to slow and even stop on occasion. I found I could communicate with plants. Not that there was a lot to be said, but I could sense their stress and also their joy in being alive. And I felt their awareness of me, which was remarkable. I began journaling as a means of communicating with my Light and discovered She loves my story and has no interest in quashing it in any way. Her evaluation of my human self is consistently kind and compassionate. Not flattering or fake, but insightful. Knowing I am a filter for what comes through, I take these messages lightly, which feels easy and appropriate. I'm not talking to 'God' but interacting with the part of me not limited to this realm. A part I value and want to connect with.

When I feel **the right now in a big way** by moving my attention to my heart and the Light which radiates out from there, it's **all systems go**. Our energy can blossom like a rose. A massive one. There is no boundary where we end and something else begins. The Animating Force wants to reveal itself; it wants to show us the underlying foundation of this transitory reality. The mystery is thrilled to meet us and this force exists everywhere. Not only in biologically living organisms but in every atom around us. This is why a friendship with your car makes it run better. Why greeting your home is a good thing to do. There isn't a single thing in our reality not alive with the energy that creates worlds. You want a satisfying life? Awaken to this possibility and let strange, magical things happen for you.

Exit the Waiting Place

In his book, *Oh the Places You'll Go*, Dr. Seuss describes a most useless place, the waiting place.

...for people just waiting. Waiting for a train to go or a bus to come, or a plane to go or the mail to come, or the rain to go or the phone to ring, or the snow to snow or waiting around for a Yes or a No or waiting for their hair to grow.
Everyone is just waiting.

The waiting place is useless because it discounts the present moment. Our attention is on what we hope is coming and this feeds disinterest in what is. We project ourselves into a future but never arrive, splintering our existence and a fractured consciousness perceives differently.

Eckhart Tolle addressed this issue by saying, "Waiting is a state of mind, the usual state of mind. Presence is when you're no longer waiting for the next moment, believing that the next moment will be more fulfilling than this one." How do we stop believing the next moment will be more satisfying? How do we stop projecting and arrive?

In asking these questions I come to a complete stop. As I sit here in front of my computer, light is falling upon me and touching my face. A car is driving through slush on the street outside; a neighbor's dog is barking, a plant beside me grows. My lungs are taking in air. My heart is beating. Here for this moment, I'm not waiting for anything. When I summon *all of me* to the present and stay there, I step from one world into another. I can only feel this awareness when I'm all in, when my every chip is on the table for this hand, when the past and future have fallen off the landscape of my attention and the whole of my existence is the breath I am taking. To discover all you ever wanted in a now moment, is to stop believing the future holds something that is missing and realize the only necessary element for a magical life is the unfractured consciousness of YOU.

Franz Kafka described it this way: *"You do not need to leave your room. Remain sitting at your table and listen. Do not even listen, simply wait. Do not even wait, be quite still and solitary. The world will freely offer itself to you to be unmasked. It has no choice; it will roll in ecstasy at your feet."*

Much of our growth comes to us a little bit at time. We take one small step, followed by another and gradually move ourselves into better places. But this particular unfolding lends itself to a big step, a leap in fact, for to feel the world roll in ecstasy at your feet is monumental. The unmasking is dramatic and the metamorphosis stunning. A paradigm shift, our capacity for awareness expands and there is no going back. Every moment forward may not be whole, but we'll know it could be. And this discernment will call us to fully inhabit the sentence we're reading, the apple we're tasting, the song we're singing, the hug we're giving. It will entice us to exit the waiting place and establish residence in the unrivaled now.

A Bridge Back to Here

Everywhere I look I see people who don't want to be here. They don't want to die, exactly, but they don't want to be here. And it's not only apparent in their addictive patterns, it's apparent in everyday ways: self-distractive tendencies, shallowing of breath and perspective, perpetual positivity, the transcendence bypass, to name a few. There are billions of ways to leave the moment. I often wonder, what has to happen before we can co-create a world that invites us to be here, truly here? And how can we construct that world if we have already left it? Where is the bridge back to here?

~ Jeff Brown

The impulse to withdraw is widespread and I want to consider the dynamics of this. What is going on? If our moments hold the possibility of bliss, why do we find a billion ways to leave them? What is off here? Two possibilities come to mind. The first is we're so convinced content is **the** defining factor for satisfaction, our minds relentlessly chase after a better story. Fixated on both past and future, this isn't a joyful pursuit but a desperate one. The second is present moment awareness is an *in-body,* not an *out-of-body* experience and our bodies hold unresolved emotions. When we stop running, our pain catches up to us, and we're alarmed by this. We haven't learned how to let our Light hold the shadows, so we protectively keep distance between us and a full perception of our right now. We don't want to feel what our body is holding, and such reluctance drives our ambivalence about this human enterprise.

Our Story-self is small and no matter what we've been programmed to believe, she doesn't have the power to fix what's wrong. She feels the pain and it comes right back. She improves her lot and remains unfulfilled. What she thinks is a step forward is a step nowhere. This is not disheartening news but crucial information. Our Light could not be closer to us than it is. Permeating every particle of our being, it simply asks us to open, to connect, to yield. And when we do, nothing is beyond Her capacity to handle. Not erase or transcend but hold and heal, which means the harm did happen but we're able to carry it and carry on. The key for me was to stop asking my Light to unhuman me, which opened the door to the merging I desired.

Allowing and awareness build a bridge back to here. At times my need for a pleasing, pain-free story is like a boomerang, circling back no matter how many times I chuck it away. But I remind myself the declaration *it's okay to be human in a human place* applies. Presence offers the well-being I long for, and it doesn't matter if I step on and off this path a thousand times a day. The Light invites me to stay.

That Which Cannot Disappoint

The things that are common to you, like windy mornings, starry skies, and old trees; beetles, strawberries, and doorbells; coffee, blue jeans, and summertime . . . are not common to us. Enjoy every flippin' moment.
~ *Notes from The Universe* by Mike Dooley

In the movie *Steel Magnolias*, the central character, Shelby, declares she would rather have thirty minutes of wonderful than a lifetime of nothing special. Her greatest desire is to have a child but health concerns mean the choice to do so may end her life and (spoiler alert) that is what happens. This touching story reveals both the futility in playing it safe and the immense value of our brief time here. But Shelby's assertion that much of life is nothing special warrants consideration.

I'm reminded of the admonition William Martin offers in his book *The Parent's Tao Te Ching*:

"Do not ask your children to strive for extraordinary lives. Such striving may seem admirable, but it is the way of foolishness. Help them instead to find the wonder and the marvel of an ordinary life. Show them the joy of tasting tomatoes, apples and pears. Show them how to cry when pets and people die. Show them the infinite pleasure in the touch of a hand. And make the ordinary come alive for them. The extraordinary will take care of itself."

Extraordinary moments (like getting married or having a child) tend to activate the energy of awareness and so we long to have them. They inspire presence and feel remarkable. Living for such milestones, however, is like repeatedly rejecting dinner for dessert and thinking you made a wise choice. When we chase highs, we live in lows. A lifetime of nothing special comes when we hold the limiting belief only exceptional moments are transcendent, when in fact every moment viewed with awareness is incredible. Life's pinnacles are gifts but so are its valleys and today there will be a thousand seemingly insignificant miracles in my life.

Awareness breathes life into the ordinary and elevates the common into that which cannot disappoint. I'm going to repeat this statement with an underline: <u>Awareness elevates the common into that which cannot disappoint.</u> When I feel empty or let down what's missing is never a something but a someone (myself), as the fulfillment I long for invariably comes through me and not to me.

Road Report: When I make the ordinary come alive (by feeling the right now in a big way), incredible things happen all the time. A video of a photographer interacting with a Great Gray Owl came across one of my social media feeds. The artist was in Yellowstone Park and spent close to an hour interacting with this remarkable bird. Heading to our family cabin for a fall weekend, I told my husband I didn't even know such owls lived in this area and wouldn't it be amazing if we saw one? As we turned a corner on Red Rock Road (not three miles from our cabin), there was a Great Gray Owl. Perched on a snow marker mere feet away, he was one chill dude - looking at us, looking around, then looking at us again. Three vehicles stopped to check him out and he never flew away. My mind was blown and my weekend made!

Then yesterday, one of our neighbor's chickens flew into our yard and wandered around for hours. A colorful rooster, he is gorgeous but it was the reaction of our cat to his presence that beat all. Alarmed, Morty would come into the house, look at us with wide eyes and I swear if he could talk, he'd have said, "Guys – an enormous bird is hanging out in our yard! What are we going to do about it?!" And although we went out to look at the chicken with him, his shocked reaction remained. It was the best! A few months back I decided to revise my simple reason for existing. I'm no longer just here for the popcorn, but here for the animals as well.

Where Can't We Go?

My parents are getting up in years and resisting change (like moving to a smaller home with no acreage) and I get it. One day you're seventy years old, you blink and turn eighty. The realization our story is coming to its end happens faster than we can assimilate and we find ourselves clinging to the trappings of a life well lived. Nostalgic, we recall the best of what's happened and fear the fading of our Light. Upon our death, the memory of us is tenuously held by our loved ones until they too expire and we are all no more. But what if there was a less disheartening actuality in play here? An actuality without loss?

I came across an assertion once which stated nothing is further away than five minutes ago. Based on the premise time is linear, the argument is once it passes, it's gone for good. From my place in the game, this is true. The clock on my computer reads 9:07 a.m. and when the last number turns to eight, the part of me focused here won't be returning there, ever. But what about the parts of me existing in different realities? Do the same rules apply?

Einstein described time as a stubbornly persistent illusion and of all the radical ideas I've ever fixated upon, few have shifted my perception of reality more than the notion time is **not** linear. Everything is happening now. Every past, every future, every possibility, every unfolding exists in a singular moment. And the Light we are owns all of it. It belongs to us, so every page in our story can be read as many times and in as many ways as we'd like. <u>Nothing is ever lost because it hasn't gone somewhere our Light</u>

<u>can't go.</u> I'm not certain what our stories look like in the other realms but I am convinced my Light can put Her favorite songs on repeat forever.

A Second Chance Day

There is a game I play that encourages me to merge the energy of awareness with my ownership of time. I call it a Second Chance Day and pretend I've returned to relive a single day in my current incarnation. From outside of time, I decide my Light has hit the repeat button and is playing it again.

Most Octobers, our family travels to a theme park in Utah called Lagoon. One year I decided to make this outing a Second Chance Day. We usually keep an eye on the weather forecast and choose accordingly, but this particular October was a busy one. We found ourselves with one available weekend and a cold, rainy forecast. It wasn't ideal for a visit to an amusement park but we decided to go anyway.

When it comes to tolerating weather extremes, I'm not a good sport. I've never been to an airshow because the prospect of high temperatures, burning sun, no shade and hot pavement keeps me away. I even passed on an Adam Lambert concert once because the venue was outdoors, in Las Vegas, in July. I've never gone midnight sledding because it is freaking cold and I would rather be asleep in a warm bed. No plans are in the works to ditch my preferences but it is said those who have the good sense to go inside when it rains miss out on a world of loveliness. My aim is not to reject my inclinations but to cultivate an attitude up for adventure; the kind of mindset I suspect I would have if I were coming back to revisit my life, if I were living a Second Chance Day.

As we pulled into the parking lot at Lagoon, the weather was crap. On a typical, first-time-around outing, I'm certain I would have complained and wished things were different. But this was no ordinary day, for I was time-traveling, returning to an ended story which meant a burning desire to embrace life bubbled up and fully eclipsed any impulse to reject it. How lucky I felt to be with my family; to be exactly where I was, when I was, as I was.

Chilly perfection surrounded me and I drank in the colors of Autumn as if I were seeing them for the first and last time. How sweet it was to come back to Halloween, with spook alleys, costumes and the Monster Mash song. The rain was refreshing, making the world soft and sagebrush-scented and lent a whole new sensation to the roller coaster rides. Wearing my puffiest coat, winter hat and gloves, I laughed with my teenagers as they gave me a hard time, saying I looked like the bundled-up kid from *A Christmas Story*. Intense pleasure arose as I tuned in to each of my children, marveling at the miracle of their existence. I found myself watching my husband, seated on benches, appreciating anew what a good sport he is. He gets sick on rides and so spends the day holding our stuff, enjoying treats and people-watching. I discovered food is better on a Second Chance Day for each sip of hot chocolate, bite of caramel apple, and French fry dipped in fry sauce provided ample reason for joy.

Everything about the day felt precious to me and nothing bothersome seemed important at all. Joni Mitchell shared wisdom with these lyrics, "Don't it always seem to go that you don't know what you've got till it's gone?" Judgments of inadequacy are common when we don't sense the value in what we have. Living a Second Chance Day is to know loss and restoration simultaneously, to leave our life and come back with greater discernment. This particular example is a bit heavy because of how I approached it. But I've learned to take this game lightly. Its purpose isn't to feel like everything I love is gone and I've momentarily got it back but to expand my capacity to show up and cherish this incredible human adventure.

Advance or Retreat

Story fatigue – it's everywhere. We think we're exhausted because we have too much to do or nothing to do we actually want to do, and both concerns are legitimate. But these aren't the reasons we're tired. The quality of our life depends on the degree of presence we bring to it and I'm not talking correlation but causation here. Life energy flows from the Animating Force, from our Light and when our source is constricted, we run on fumes.

We unknowingly obstruct the channels through which life energy animates us. Disaffected, heavily yoked and living small, it's no surprise we're depleted. Under such conditions, how could it be otherwise? Life turns into dinner at a cheap buffet, our plates overloaded with too many tasteless entrees we have no desire to eat. Stuck, we see no physical way to leave the table, so we make a mental exit instead. Checking out is a common coping mechanism, revealing the desire to escape reality. <u>Here</u>, but not <u>here enough</u> to feel good, our withdrawal is understandable. But such impulses can also serve as wake-up calls precipitating awareness. When I want to retreat (and this happens daily), I can open the closed channels by looking closer at why I want to leave reality and reconsider my approach.

Disaffection – Our minds are prone to quash life energy for they stand in opposition to so much and that's a retreat every time. This is not just the spoiling-for-a-fight resistance my mind chooses on social media, but a disaffection with life itself. The luster is lost and that impression is draining.

Humans of New York highlighted a physician mother who took some flak for sharing she found caring for her infant tedious and did not want to be a stay-at-home mom. Her husband had chosen to give primary care to their son so she could do the healing work she felt called to do. I found her honesty refreshing. We conflate loving our children with the tasks of parenting, but what part of sleepless nights, dirty diapers, tantrums, messes, sibling fights, homework, sass, and irrational meltdowns makes for a good time? Yes, there are sweet hugs, bedtime stories and tuck-ins, laughter, celebrations, all the first experiences and countless moments we would not trade. But like everything in this world, raising children is both misery and joy. No doubt being a doctor is the same.

A friend and her husband discovered a passion for biking around the same time their business was struggling. The thrill they felt while riding pulled them into their life during a time fear might have caused them to retreat. Bike riding is a full engagement activity and so pushes us to pay attention. And when we do, we feel enlivened. We need hobbies like this because they tip the scales in favor OF life. It's likely we have work that frustrates us; situations that challenge us; chores we'd like to pass on. Life is a mixed bag and no amount of money or positive thinking changes this. My desire to retreat lessens when I stop demanding a utopia to inhabit and let my Light show me how to love a garden with weeds. The gift of awareness is affection for life, in all its complexity. What matters then isn't so much **what** I'm doing but **how much of me** I'm doing it with.

Heavily Yoked — One of my great-grandmothers raised eleven children during the Depression. When asked how she managed, she replied nothing is hard while you're doing it. A single task is always manageable but this requires living in the present moment and our minds seek complications. Past and future concerns make for a heavy burden and we only get out from under their yoke when we consciously set them down and live in the now.

All day long I attempt to leap a whole flight of stairs instead of taking one at a time. And it's tiresome. I mentally prepare an entire dinner instead of washing a single potato. When I'm deciding what to make for dinner, I schlepp resentment (for having to make such decisions since the dawn of time) along with me. Not fun. When I write, the scale of an entire book bears down on me and turns the completion of a single sentence into a burdensome task. I worry about situations that have nothing to do with my right now - longing to rectify some past hurt or preemptively prevent harm from coming. This unsettling approach is suffocating, extracting oxygen from the room until it's hard to breathe. It's no wonder I'm weary.

A yoke was a wooden crosspiece placed over the backs of animals and people - representing bondage, oppression, subjugation – and this image packs a punch. But the heaviness of time is self-imposed and I am free to cast it off at will. No one has put this upon me. As an empowered being, I can choose to be where my feet are, aware in this moment, traveling lightly.

Living Small — Friend, I've given much thought to the processing system that is the whole of us (our Light) and hope by this point, you know exactly what I mean by *a big way*. This is so critically important I'm going address it again. We live small when our consciousness is held to the faculties of mind. This operating mode could be compared to having a disease where the body is unable to absorb nutrients. Food is present but passes through our digestive system unutilized. Even though our Light is right here, we can't avail ourselves of it and end up soul-tired.

When I live through my whole energy body and assimilate my story from there, all desire to check out ceases. I get my mind is neither an enemy nor an answer. It doesn't need to be banished or bettered, but put in the proper order of things. WHO we really are comes first and is worth a dogged pursuit for here's the thing: reality sucks us dry when we live small.

For me, this dogged pursuit isn't a grueling challenge, but a bone I refuse to drop. It is a constant reminder to GO BIG right now. This choice starts as a movement (from my mind to my heart) and travels out from there. I feel myself as a brilliant being of Light, a radiating mass of energy, an unconsumable flame. This Light pulses in every cell of my body. It is in the cup I am holding, the birds I am watching, the music floating around my kitchen. Pervasive and profound, it meets me in the eyes of every person I encounter. Friend, I wish I could address you by name and implore you to join me in not settling for small. We can live soul touched instead of tired, set alight and woven into a world of magic.

Road Report: Last night was Halloween and as we were headed to bed, my husband thanked me for handling the shit detail of answering the door all evening to give out candy while he watched the world series. I did miss the game but I didn't mind. When I choose to really show up for this holiday, I'm bowled over by its generosity and goodwill. I love my community and our kids are awesome. We get mostly junior high age (as the younger ones go to a trunk or treat), who are friendly and appreciative. Hands down, the best moment this year was getting to give a dog treat to a good boy named White Chicken who was over-the-top thrilled to be out adventuring with his humans and their pack of friends.

Residency

When we live without awareness, we seek distractions, short-lived pleasures, and numbing activities to soothe ourselves. Heads barely above water, we don't want to face the fact we're struggling to swim. It could be unresolved pain, stifling boredom, nagging disappointment, or a survival mountain we're hard-pressed to climb. Cue the craving for our drug of choice and the relief it offers.

We're all familiar with addictions and how they run the gamut from life-destroying to merely annoying (like a fly which keeps landing on you). Maybe the energy of awareness could set one free from an addiction with its hands on your throat in a chokehold but I have no first-hand experience with that. I do know the crux of a twelve-step program is to turn our life over to a power greater than ourselves (the Light as we understand it) and any restoration to sanity may hinge on our ability to do so.

Addressing the "annoying fly type" of addiction is relevant to awareness, however. For what is an addiction if not a means of escape? A distraction from discomfort? A method of retreat? There is a MASH episode where the character Radar drinks some of Hawkeye's homemade gin and complains, "I thought this stuff was supposed to make you feel better," to which Hunnicutt responds, "No, it's supposed to make you feel nothing." Do we fix ourselves a cocktail because we find life dismal or because rum and coke is a lovely thing to enjoy? Is a bowl of ice cream a delicious treat we're savoring or a fast track to feeling numb? Do we watch television programs to see a photographer give scritches to a shark (in *Tales by Light*) or to fill the empty hours? Is the phone that never leaves our hands telling us a story about alligators who rescued a dog or providing a place to go so we don't have to be here?

Anything can operate addictively. For me, the telling question and answer is this: does what I'm doing feel good before, during and after? Addictions have uncomfortable energies attached to them; they feel disempowering (you can't stop), needy (desire for more and more), and shaming (hiding your behavior from yourself and others). Plus, there is usually some hangover effect. Whenever there is a downside, I can be certain awareness is lacking and I'm focusing small.

Another way to look at addiction is to see how it sells momentary pleasure at a high cost. Like buying a single Hershey's Kiss for a hundred dollars – brief chocolate bliss followed by an empty bank account (because you won't stop with one). The solution isn't to go cold turkey and give up chocolate forever, or find a more affordable source, or replace it with a treat you can better control. Awareness isn't swapping highly destructive behaviors for less destructive ones. People fall off the wagon because it's a white-knuckling unpleasant ride. We aren't looking to replace something that feels good with nothing but replace a flash of relief with a column of Light.

We become the source of our own satisfaction and that is an unrivalled position from which to play this game. For when we **go big**, the things that were check-outs - become check-ins. I joke I'm addicted to gardening but there is no downside - just this crazy, passionate affection I feel for plants.

To others my choices might look out of balance, but presence doesn't mean behaving reasonably. It means coming at life from a position of wholeness and there is no set script that follows. I am being encouraged by my Light to scale this hobby back a bit because I'm no longer a spring chicken but an autumn hen. And I don't need a huge garden to experience huge magic. We are the only ones who know if our choices reflect expansion or retraction; if we are establishing residency in or vacating our life.

The Rapture of Being Alive

People say that what we're all seeking is a meaning for life. I don't think that that's what we're really seeking. I think that <u>what we're seeking is an experience of being alive,</u> so that our life experiences on the purely physical plane will have resonance within our own innermost being and reality, so that we can actually feel the rapture of being alive.
~ Joseph Campbell

While visiting with a counselor, an older woman shared her regret in not living true to herself and her dreams. She'd chosen a traditional path advised by others but wished she'd have dated women, gotten tattoos and explored the world from the seat of a motorcycle. How sweet are the energies of adventure and freedom? Can't you picture this woman on a bike with her girlfriend caught up in the rapture of being alive? I wish I could package such emotions and deliver them to every person on this planet. But the truth is, that parcel has been in our possession from the moment we arrived here. Because rapture isn't a girlfriend, a tattoo, and a motorcycle (or in my case a corgi, a camper and a kayak,) it's our Light. We chase after trappings looking for something we already own.

A remarkable tv program called *The Magical Andes*, highlights the largest flying bird in the world, the Andean Condor. Described as a life-changing experience, should I ever have the astounding good fortune to see one in flight, I know I'll be overcome with the rapture of being alive. Because I will 100% show up for that experience. The nudge here isn't to plan a trip to South America (although it's made my bucket list) but connect with the beauty around me; to uncover my Light first and let it reveal I'm surrounded by Andean Condors. I'll concede that everything isn't quite so exquisite, but it's close enough to nullify any fear of missing out or sense of regret.

C.S. Lewis said, *"We do not want merely to see beauty. We want something else which can hardly be put into words – to be united with the beauty we see, to pass into it, to receive it into ourselves, to bathe in it, to become part of it."* This is what the energy of awareness offers, an epiphany we are already inside the borders of staggering beauty. Incomparable love is the connecting core of all that is, so to suppose we are outside looking in, is to be ignorant of our true nature. Feeling the right now in a big way, isn't an alchemy of becoming but of perceiving what already is.

A rapturous life is not some rare gift, enjoyed by a lucky few who are doing extraordinary things but an inherent potential for each of us that will present itself when **we** do.

It Will Show up when We Do

This idea feels like an appropriate ending note for the energy of awareness, as I'm convinced everything we truly want shows up when **we** do. And by **we,** I mean our merged Story/Light self. And by **it,** I mean the height of human experience. Our Light is the repository of all good things — She is every energy we want to explore here.

We find freedom, not because we leave our story but because we invite our Light and Her liberty into it. We find abundance, not because we dismiss our limited identity but because we include our Light and the plenty which attends Her. We find peace, not because we force our will upon reality (and turn it into something more palatable) but because we merge with our Light and come away intact. This is not a fully awakened position but a blended one. Awareness is letting the fog of disconnection gently burn away. It is opening the windows to Light and fresh air. It is learning not to silence our stories but let them speak.

Some spiritual paths promote a full awakening while in our human state and for a long time I believed that was my endgame. But the more I looked for universal answers, the more I uncovered personal ones. And the longer I play this game the more convinced I become we aren't all here for the same reason. If we are each a micro-God creating our own Universe, then our purpose is our call.

My Light has never encouraged me (a Story-self) to go away but stick around. Even when I am fed up and disheartened over my humanness, She insists on riding shotgun. She's along to offer direction (plus a lot of encouragement and support) but refuses to take the wheel. This is my path, my moving target of truth today. Right now, I am here for the animals and the merging. I know it would feel better if I were nothing but Light and I suspect that is a choice I'm making in many realities. But it is not the choice I am making in this one.

THREE

The Energy of Support

In the midst of winter, I found there was,
within me, an invincible summer.
~ Albert Camus, ***The Stranger***

What would it be like to live in a world that held you? That reached for your hand and walked beside you? That carried burdens and tended hurts? That answered questions and offered peace? That shifted perspective while nudging you in helpful directions? What would it be like to live in a world where a push from the nest only proved you could fly? Where contrast was more of a launch than a kick? Where a sea-worthy vessel provided transport throughout this rough-and-tumble voyage?

It's concerning I have to stretch a bit to imagine this. That such focus isn't my default setting. My rational mind argues a mountain of evidence proves this world is godforsaken territory, so why would support be my go-to position? But how do I know an exceedingly supportive reality could not exist or that it doesn't already? What if my persistence in stockpiling confirmation of a harsh world was the deciding factor as to the reality I inhabit? What if an invincible summer was lacking only because I'd put so little effort into finding it?

These considerations push me toward accountability. Not heavy-handed blame, but a gentle acknowledgment that I'll never know my power until I pull the sword from the stone, direct my attention, and find the King Arthur inside me. A God Force incarnate, I have influence here. Too often, though, I fail to connect the dots of my reality back to their point of origin – my focus. In no way am I asserting reality is simple. It is not. Its complexity and attendant pain are why the energy of support is needed.

I want to live in a reality where support abounds and I'm immersed in it. To feel the sun behind every cloud, no matter what. To be warmed by a source that doesn't cool because I turned away. I want my metaphysical address to be: *Julie Merrick – currently inhabiting an exceptionally kind and supportive reality.* Steadfast backing from a loving Universe is no longshot gamble but a sure thing. Let's roll the dice.

A Compassionate Energy

Support is an energy I've explored from many angles. What did I think it was and what was it really? The fact that it comes both <u>through us and to us</u> and what this means. How support plays out in the best and worst of times, for both significant and relatively insignificant challenges. Friend, I ask you to be sensitive to where you are in a moment of reading. If reality has pulled a rug out from under you and left you reeling, skip over the fluff. It won't be of much help. We all face dark nights of the soul, when we question the presence of Light and if it will even help us. The idea of suggesting how to find support in the hardest of times seems presumptuous. There are burdens I will not carry in this Life; mountains I won't climb, adversities I will not face. Struggles I cannot fully understand. Knowing this, a self-serving impulse pushes me to avoid saying much so as not to offend. But how much support is in such a cowardly choice? I wish I could reach into your Life and undo any harm there - that I could rewind, erase, or offer you a pen to write a story without suffering. But this game doesn't work that way for any of us.

My journey is all I have to draw from, and there are two things I feel to offer before you read any further. First, my own experience with hurt has taught me Life can take my anger (or despair) and it will stick around. It's okay to get mad at Life. It understands and it listens. Aim your darkest feelings straight at the source that put you here. Fire those bullets and when the chambers are empty, put down your gun, feel the depth of your pain and surrender to the shitshow our stories can be. I don't know if "it's all good," but I do know such claims strike me as superficial and dismissive. My acceptance of whatever is, reveals a power continuously by my side. A force which hears what I need to express and never discounts my perceptions of my own experience.

My second offering is also a request. Friend, if you've survived a dark night and lived to greet the dawn, I ask you to lend a hand here. To pause for a moment and feel your part in this connection. I think of us as kith and kin and though we may not understand each other's lives completely, we understand enough. Support is a compassionate energy that travels unhindered across time. Our Story-self can physically help those near us on the path, but our merged Story-Light self has a more extended reach. We can hold each other in compassion, bearing burdens to soften blows, accepting and releasing collective pain in a way that serves humanity. Yielding on behalf of another is not enabling or embodying the world's suffering but bringing our Light to the collective.

What follows next is my on-the-ground take of how support comes through us. Practical stuff but also what I suggest skipping over if you're hurting. My Light is adamant I repeat this point: a Universe exists that wants only to hug and hold us through whatever we're facing. We are never alone and we are not unknown.

Support Coming Through Us

Opting In

On rare occasions, I've been out to dinner with people who did not tip or tipped far less than is customary (and it had nothing to do with quality of service). Shocked, this struck me as so detrimental to being supported I could not fathom any justification for it. Our actions are crucial in expanding or diminishing energy fields, and we cannot withdraw our support from others without reality withdrawing its support for us. The creative medium does not reward or punish through some scale reading of right and wrong - it simply reflects. If I behave miserly, callously, or indifferently, then these conditions are mirrored in my experience. If I behave generously, thoughtfully, or respectfully, these states will be echoed back to me. The choice to see and value others is the choice to be seen and valued ourselves.

Delving into how this works, I began to see the energy of support was not as straightforward as I'd supposed. Many of my assumptions required scrutiny. Foremost was the belief that support is a balancing energy. Surprisingly, it's not. It's <u>a participatory one.</u> We don't earn our way in - we opt-in. I'd thought of it like a checking account that required deposits so there'd be funds to draw upon and also a tip twenty percent to get a twenty percent return kind of interplay. But there is no order of operations where we must give first in order to receive. No running balance can be added to or subtracted from. No obligation to pay it forward or pay it back.

In the energy of support, the dynamics of giving and receiving are **inseparable**. One function never exists apart from the other. I cannot emphasize this point enough - other energies are in play when giving or getting stand-alone.

Getting by itself

Getting by itself is wanting something for nothing and indicates a belief in scarcity. Exposing insecurity, *getting by itself* is certain there is not enough to go around. Steeped in competition, *getting by itself* approaches abundance like a zero-sum game. We take, hoard, and cling to an artificial state of well-being that arises when our gain comes through another's loss. We cannot be at ease.

Besting others may seem advantageous on the surface (more money in our pockets, for example), but any in-depth evaluation would reveal the creation of private hells. Harsh, such disconnect plays itself out along every point of the economic spectrum. Hold any billionaire (who made their fortune through capitalism) in mind and see what you discover by sensing the energy they actually live in.

It's said karma is a bitch but energy has no lag time. A fortune earned by impoverishing people and harming our planet can pay for a lot of distraction, but it cuts connection off at the knees. This is not meant to be a moral judgment but a reality check. We can't pull thievery from the shelf and serve ourselves support for dinner. Billionaires are an easy target, but disconnect is rampant and the entire lot of us are mired in its toxic effects. Friend, it is discouraging when I see my own feet in this muck and disheartening when my micro-movements toward connection seem too small to make much difference. But my Light counsels me to calm down and stop catastrophizing. We've not been assigned to save the world but choose the parameters of our own story.

So, let me approach this concern from a more proximate angle. In reviewing a credit card statement, a refund was issued for two photo books I'd given as Christmas presents. The transaction was no longer the done deal I'd thought it was and annoyance tempted me to justify doing nothing.

Internal arguments for opting out: *They made a mistake and I shouldn't have to hassle with it. It's not a lot of money and it's not a big deal. It's January and I'm tired.*

Internal arguments for opting in: *It is a big deal because choosing to do nothing will weaken my connection to humanity. It will distance me from Life.*

My response was an opportunity to close the gap and draw nearer to Life. I was pleased with the quality of the books and impressed with the company (Mixbook). I found their website intuitive, their prices affordable and their shipping fast. This business mattered (competent or not) and this fact was mine to see or to ignore.

Opting in, what I thought would be a bother, wasn't. It took me all of one minute to send an email thanking them for their service, explaining the error and asking how best to proceed. They responded promptly, thanking me for being a customer and sharing their policy of not recharging when a glitch like this happens. The interaction was agreeable. Had they rerun the charge, this would have satisfied me as well. An unexpected windfall came my way but I felt no compulsion to order more books to make things right. Things were already right.

A defining characteristic of support is whatever happens feels appropriate and affirming – in all directions. *Getting by itself* feels off because it is. Detrimental, it is helping oneself to office goodies but never bringing anything to share; it's commuting with a coworker on their dime; it's accepting a shoulder to lean on but never providing one. Bankrupt, it is manipulating others to get what we want and creates impoverished stories strapped for Light.

Road Report: Last night while enjoying a dinner out, our waitress heavily pushed the nightly special. Super enthusiastic, she assured us four orders had already been placed, they'd likely run out soon and it was an option we wouldn't want to miss. My husband doesn't care for scallops but I ordered them. The dish did not live up to her hype and cost twice as much as anything else on the menu (I hadn't thought to ask.) It was an expensive, disappointing meal. A situation I'd usually shrug off, it kept coming to mind. This morning as I sat down to write, I realized why. She was being manipulative and the interaction felt neither appropriate or affirming. I would not label her a "bad" person, but someone who has bought into the ideology that shrewd people use duplicity to gain advantage. Do what you must to close the deal, complete the sale, come out on top, or get a bigger tip.

Friend, I'm not sharing this story with you because I think you hold such opinions. In fact, I'd bet the farm you are nowhere near such energy. I share this example because such choices stem from ignorance and elicit my compassion. Micro-movements toward support and connection have placed me in a reality so meaningful watching a dove bed down in one of our feeders (after unloading a forty-pound bag of seed from my car) overwhelms me with a sense of belonging. Disconnect is so painful by comparison we would not choose it knowingly. This is the reminder I need to look to my own experience for truth and not be fooled by the fragmented hype that the more we take, the more we'll have.

Support is a circle of abundance with two entry requirements. First, we displace no one to be there. And second, we set aside all attempts to earn our way in - which brings up the subject of righteousness.

Giving by Itself

Driven by a belief in righteousness, *giving by itself* is striving to establish virtue, build up an identity of value, and prove our worthiness. It may seem odd that any type of giving could be antithetical to the energy of support, but *giving by itself* is. Righteousness and self-righteousness are indistinguishable states of being and what they create is destructive. Relentlessly judgmental, both inward and outward, such energy dims our Light.

When pursuing righteousness, I question all my choices and task myself with acts of kindness. I strive to do good deeds, worry if I've paid it forward, doubt if I've done enough. When I'm pursuing righteousness, I judge what others give, what others take, and how they choose to live. Everything I observe slides under a microscope of holiness, revealing fault. If you're chasing it down, it isn't support. If you're calculating its value, it isn't support. If you're broadcasting it for the world to see, it isn't support. If you fear an accounting followed by a reckoning, it isn't support.

That last sentence is a bit *'sinners in the hands of an angry God'* and your religious background may be nothing like mine. But for Americans in particular, our shared puritanical heritage exalts giving while condemning human nature as selfish and we suffer as a result. Detached, we scramble to be what we've forgotten we are: connected. When we choose to opt in, support feels untroubled.

One spring, a pair of reclining camp chairs were tagged at a yard sale near our house. The seller told us they were heavy and awkward, so we didn't buy them. As summer progressed, however, we questioned that decision. Back and forth, we discussed making such a purchase but failed to land one way or the other. Fall arrived and I found myself in a thrift store looking at similar chairs. Reasonably priced and in excellent shape, this felt like an answer to my asking. I happily pulled the tags to pay for them. Moments later, another customer rounded a corner and exclaimed to her friend these chairs were exactly what she'd been looking for! Her disappointment in realizing they were already sold gave me pause and I considered letting her have them. Isn't that what a *good* person would do? This reaction was driven by righteousness, which is dominant for me. If I'd thought *I found them first, so I win!* scarcity would have been the driver.

Outside of support, a win comes through another's loss or is exchanged for a tally on an imaginary *good* person scorecard.

Before I understood support, this is what every situation in my Life looked like. Believing scarcity and righteousness were my only options, I'd never considered how unsatisfying they are. In her book, *Dying to be Me*, Anita Moorjani explains when we know ourselves AS love, we stop trying to be loving or judge what love means. Support works the same way. There was no right or wrong choice to be made here. I could keep the chairs and be in support (the Universe would take care of her) or I could give her the chairs (and the Universe would take care of me). With no righteousness to earn or scarcity to avoid, either choice was okay. Checking in, I asked myself *what do I feel to do here*? and I decided to keep the chairs. No guilt. No waffling. No impulse to justify a selfish course of action because it wasn't. (Your level of discomfort with this decision reveals how enmeshed you are with righteousness.)

Sometimes I check in and feel to do what could be labeled generous. I happily gave a brand-new sewing machine to a friend who needed it. I could have sold it to her or someone else or kept it as the backup I originally intended but I didn't. No gold star, brownie points, or pat on the back for doing a good deed. No impulse toward self-congratulations for making a selfless decision because it wasn't. Selfish and selfless play no part in an energy of oneness.

What Support Isn't

<u>Support is not control</u>. We all have preferences as to how we want to live. Trouble comes when we decide what is best for us, is best for all. Common in relationships (particularly parent/child ones) such beliefs produce indentured energy. We sell them as supportive but they aren't. *I know best* agendas grant permission to engage in all manner of controlling behaviors. Lectures, testimonies, withheld approval, and expressed disappointment are obvious ones. But physical and financial help generates resentment if every act of giving comes wrapped in obligation. Pseudo-support feels like offering a glass of dirty water or reluctantly drinking it. Genuine support is clean and this analogy guides me. If I choose to give with expectations (even something as simple as a thank you) then what I'm offering is tainted for everyone involved.

One area in particular consistently trips me up. Most people do not care about gardens the way I do. In my opinion, we'd all benefit from hollyhocks and homegrown tomatoes. As my daughters have become adults (I have better boundaries with my daughter-in-law), I've wanted them to have lovely outdoor spaces and pushed this preference. They'd be surprised if I didn't show up each Spring and Fall with a box of bulbs and perennials, sleeves rolled up and tools in hand. Mostly, they're willing participants but I want cleaner water here. Fewer strings of any kind. Support that is more about what pleases them, than pleases me. This is definitely a *me* problem. My children joke their father and I should move so I'll have a new yard to fix up. I commandeer their space for my passion and tell myself I'm being supportive.

This particular *me* problem is complicated but we can narrow its' scope. It is possible to filter out control by examining thoughts running in the background. Thoughts like: *I bought the most adorable books for your children, are you reading to them? I made you a flannel quilt, are you enjoying it?* And a pertinent one for the gardening example: *We worked our butts off planting these flowers, are you weeding and watering them so they'll thrive?* (Holy hell - my poor daughters. Nothing like giving someone a living gift along with the charge to keep it that way!)

Parents mean well but the energy of support gets muddied when it comes to our kids. Our good intentions go too far and healthy boundaries blur. Genuine support is blessing the lives of others not from a place of having no preferences but from a place of burdening no one with them. That is a key to filtering out control. We needn't beat up on ourselves for being human. We can do such thoughts and then undo them. Untie the strings and set everyone free. Support also leads to amnesia by keeping us in the present. What books? (Oh yeah, those were super cute! I love children's books!) What quilt? (I'd forgotten about that. It did turn out nice, didn't it?) What flowers? (Just kidding – of course I remember the flowers!)

<u>Support is not sacrifice</u>. Sacrifice is the destruction of one thing for the sake of something else. The concept originated when an imagined Deity would require the killing of a valued entity to show subservience and earn favor. Superstitious nonsense and a byproduct of extreme unconsciousness. Any God who would ask us to kill another to prove obedience is lodged in hell, not heaven. Such archaic practices may have been abandoned but residual effects remain. Self-abnegating, sacrifice demands we get on our knees and stay there. It holds us both in check and in place.

Religious dogma presents sacrifice as a pious endeavor but it inter-feres with Light and I find it repulsive. The harm we do to each other and ourselves stems from disconnection, so why promote such cutting energy? Because the more distance religion can put between us and Life, the more money, fealty and control they gain. Fasting, tithing, repentance, penance and even worship are shame-inducing sacrificial directives. The doctrine of a needful atonement for a fallen humankind is a cold and broken hallelujah—hard selling what is untrue. Love does not arise from affirming we are nothing (and God is everything) but remembering we are all God and our Light is everywhere.

You might question why I'm choosing to criticize religion and I'll tell you. Most of them serve an ounce of truth with a pound of bullshit, paying lip service to love while tearing us apart. And when they can't deliver on their promises, they claim we are at fault. The God Force I've come to know is nothing like this. The belief we must make ourselves small and suffer to be of value in this world takes us away from the Field of All Possibilities. It severs our connection with Life. The Universe doesn't go hungry so we can be fed.

Simone de Beauvoir said true generosity is <u>to give your all and feel that it cost you nothing.</u> An ever-flowing spring, support does not drain or diminish. It sustains and enhances. I don't sacrifice to create a paradise garden but give my whole heart in cultivating beauty here. I don't forsake myself for family but delight in sharing this adventure with them and want nothing more than to form a circle of support we live in together. Should I spend my entire Life working for a cause, it would not make me less, but more. Support doesn't knock itself down so another can rise. It doesn't forfeit its value in the interest of humility (or humanity). And it would never sanction destruction for a greater good.

<u>Support is not charity.</u> The Bible defines charity as the pure love of Christ, but it strikes me as another form of righteousness that isn't loving at all. A story was told about a family who'd lost their father and were going through hard times. When the church they attended announced a drive to collect funds for a needy family, the youngest daughter was excited to contribute. She and her sister worked and saved. When the time came, they proudly placed their contribution into the offering plate only to have it returned to them by their minister later in the day. (Turns out theirs was the family in need.) Shamed and embarrassed, the daughter declared she would never attend church again. The next Sunday came around and her mother insisted they go. When the minister announced a new drive to collect money for poor people in another country, the family happily donated the money they'd received, glad for how rich they were in Jesus. (They were uncomfortable being the recipients of charity but I guess other people like it?!)

Good grief, how do we not see this kind of giving for what it is? Prosperity gospel at its finest. God blesses the righteous, the worthy, the best people. If you are poor, you are less than others - not as capable, not as favored, not as obedient, not as valued, and probably not as white. Charity carries a message of superiority/inferiority. *There but for the grace of God go I.* On the surface, this saying seems to express humility, but does it? Why did God grace you and not someone else? I once attended a catholic mass where the entire service was a promise from God to grant you prosperity while destroying your enemies. What the actual hell?

Humans are doing the best we can, but our evolution is in its infancy and such teachings reveal this. The energy of separation is evident everywhere we look, especially in societal structures advancing privilege for some and obstacles for others. Believing we've somehow *earned or deserve* our privilege is part of the problem. Support is not the offering of a handout or even a hand-up but the joining of hands on a journey we're taking together. It's an energy issue we're dealing with and we're all in the same boat. Given privilege, those who don't have it now would take advantage. There isn't some group of highly evolved people on this planet who need to be ferreted out and put in charge (as it wouldn't make much difference). Our collective consciousness dominates and it is where it is. The anger so many of us feel for those who disagree with us and behave differently than we think is appropriate (I'm certainly no exception here) reveals **where** we are (not **who** we are) and why we're struggling.

What can be done? Personally, the more I disconnect from contemptuous social media the better. This world doesn't need my anger or despair (no matter how justified) it needs my love. *The Light is blocked and there is no one to blame.* As a group, we're in the dark. Getting mad about this is like the overused adage of rearranging deck chairs on the Titanic. Futile. Until our collective energy shifts, we're going down. Anger may appear to drive change, but it's more of the same energy and it won't stop us sinking.

Connection reveals the astonishing Light behind every story (**who** we are) and support flourishes in its presence. When I choose connection in my own Life, as best I can, I add to its momentum. I am hopeful a tipping point will come and change the world we live in; that equitable conditions will arise and require no fight to keep in place. Until then, I don't think it's ever a mistake to help others, but if we fail to examine hand-me-down beliefs carried over from an even less evolved past, we will remain shipwrecked.

No Sacred Cows

A friend of mine helped me edit this book. She is also an ex-Mormon and questioned if it wouldn't be better to avoid criticizing religion and focus on the positive. I sat with this suggestion for a long while and couldn't digest it. I don't feel to tiptoe around sacred cows. I have no problem putting a nail in the coffin of religion when I believe its teachings are destructive. These are my truths, perceptions and understandings. Those offended are reading a book written for someone else. Not to be unwelcoming, but conversion is not my thing. It reeks of arrogance and fuels discord. Christians claim persecution whenever non-Christians set boundaries. News flash - we don't want you to witness to us. We'll have no trouble finding you if we're interested in your religion. Deep breath. Let me be kinder here. Under the thumb of indoctrination, fearful believers are blind to the religion-serving manipulation behind such directives. Convert and be converted.

My purpose here is not to disparage the beliefs of others but to share my impressions with those traveling a road similar to mine. Friends, I have come to this conclusion: I hold ingrained beliefs that impede energies I want to live in and oblivious positivity is no remedy. Courage is acknowledging we made a cake with salt instead of sugar and no sunny declaration *but the frosting is good* is sound reason to keep eating it. Support is an energy my religious upbringing mucked up and I needed to clean the stalls. I couldn't understand why I felt so much internal conflict over a practice as seemingly positive as giving and these explorations provided answers. When control, sacrifice and charity are set aside, what remains is exquisitely life-affirming.

Support Coming to Us

An Astonishing Light

I wish I could show you when you are alone or in the darkness,
the astonishing Light of your own being.
~ Hafiz of Perez

I am confident there are other dimensions in time and space, realities in addition to this one but what can I really know? A goldfish in a bowl is not capable of understanding the larger world of which he's part and how relevant would such knowledge even be? It would make no difference in the fish's Life, so I question if my theories about the unseen world matter. I think they do. Human beliefs are meaningful because they build the house we live in. We cannot *know* with certainty what is out there while existing here, but we can ponder our subjective opinions and assess what they create.

I choose to believe this human game is about God wanting to live a story. A billion, billion stories in fact. Stories that are not being micro-managed by some personage on a throne. Everything in existence is born from a Field of All Possibilities. A Field with no limits and no agenda. A reality like ours is desirable because there are no stories IN the Field. There is bliss; there is rest; there is peace; there is a love beyond anything we've felt here, but there are no stories. When loved ones die, the possibility they've gone to a better place is comforting. I think we return to the Field, which could be compared to the best sleep imaginable and something we all need on a regular basis. But once we're rested and restored, we want to get up, gather our things and head out on a new adventure.

God is willing to trade safety for a story because the exchange is fictitious. There is no danger. God is as afraid of stories as we are of dreams – they only seem like a big deal until we wake up. Oneness doesn't cease to exist when a portion of its consciousness launches itself into an expression. The love we are goes everywhere we do. When I am mindful of nature, I feel held by a vast, vibrant force which pulses with caring and compassion. My entire perception shifts and I have no adequate way to describe what I'm encountering. What I believe is this – something significant in this Universe gives a damn about us and that is a game-changer.

Multi-faceted projections from the Field, we are not one story but many. The complexity of this is beyond my ability to comprehend, but as it has little direct bearing on the choices before me, this isn't a problem. What is expedient is this: behind my story is an astonishing Light, a soul self if you will, and She has my back. Support in my Life is grounded in this belief.

Let me explain how I think this works. The Field is loving but neutral, powerful but unconcerned with what happens. Because everything happens. Diagnosed with a serious illness, in one reality we'll recover, in another we will not. Life plays itself out in every possible way. We've imagined ourselves outside the Field, but in truth, we've gone nowhere. It's a dream and there is no danger.

In the dream, however, it's a different story. The illusion is intense. There is an episode of *The Good Wife*, where Alicia's daughter, Grace, befriends a religious girl who teaches her to pray. At first, Grace is uncomfortable and protests prayer is like talking to a genie. But when her friend offers up a heartfelt petition for God to save a man's Life, the energy shifts. Grace was taken in and so was I. How meaningful is it to have something bigger than us, care for us? Someone of significance to listen and respond? To feel less alone here?

The snag, of course, is why would a God capable of intervening allow suffering? But what if that isn't how it works at all? What if support from an unseen world was more about having a friend along for the ride? A powerful one who could help us traverse the reality we find ourselves living? Guiding us to heal or to accept our own passing? Not pulling strings like a puppet master but unwaveringly with us for the journey.

I believe the Astonishing Light of my being is the holder of my story and is doing everything in Her power to let me know She is here for me. These positions I've chosen are confirmed by my experience and I like what they create. This doesn't mean I'm convinced they're absolutely true. New concepts may present themselves and persuade me to take a different path. For now, these beliefs build a house I want to live in.

A profound and expansive mystery is in play and no admonition to be rational will sway me into believing small. How can we know for certain the little fish swimming around in the little bowl, does not hold some awareness he is indeed part of a miraculous Universe?

The Entire Point

How we connect with the unseen world is our choice. The advice to embrace what resonates and release what does not, is sound as it puts us on a path that works. The idea we could communicate with our Light through writing appealed to me and is the direction I took. I'm uncomfortable with traditional religious spirituality and also that on the fringes. Honoring my preferences led me to connect in a way both comforting and intriguing.

This book is one way I've drawn on support from an unseen world to help me understand, to evolve, to delve into the mystery and return changed. Not just an upgrade to a more pleasing illusion but a shift in how I'm woven into the illusion itself. Our existence is the point. The entire point. And as every potential exists, there is no cause to diligently search out some pre-eminent meaning, trying to uncover why we are alive or what we intended to do here. We're going to do it all. We'll be born and die a day later and we'll also live to be ninety. We will meet up with thrilling success and distressing failure, impacting the world in ways both hurtful and helpful. We'll see our dreams come to fruition and we'll watch them slip away. A million miracles will happen for us but no particular unfolding is intrinsically of greater value than any other. This understanding offers tremendous freedom, for we are not singular stories but innumerable ones and the meaning of any one life is the meaning we choose. But this position also runs the risk of setting us adrift.

I'm reminded of the Joaquin Phoenix movie, *Her,* where the main character falls in love with an AI being named Samantha and becomes distraught upon learning she communicates and engages romantic relationships with countless others. Our Light fully supports each one of our many stories. From a singular perspective, this could make us feel less significant, as we're a one and not an only. The energy of connection moves me to set these concerns aside. The capacity to know and cherish each flower in a field of flowers is unbounded in their realm. I don't benefit less because my other selves are also loved.

Toast

Continually looking for the meaning of Life is like looking for the meaning of toast. It is sometimes better just to eat the toast.
~Matt Haig

I'm struggling a bit here. I want to move on to specifics of how I choose to draw on support from the unseen world. Instead, I feel like I need to pen a complete philosophy as to my take on the nature of reality and I don't have one. Not a complete one. There is a level of hurt experienced here, I'm at a loss to explain. Why would beings of Light purposefully subject themselves to extreme suffering? No adequate reason presents itself and believe me, I've asked.

Eckhart Tolle teaches if we had not suffered as we have, there would be no depth to us as human beings, no humility, no compassion. Charles Mackesy writes in *The Boy, the Mole, the Fox and the Horse,* that sometimes all you hear about is the hate, but there is more love in this world than you could imagine. These sentiments may be the closest thing to an answer I'm going to get. They move my energy. What they don't do is wrap this issue up in a neat little package that leaves me thinking, I understand.

I don't know if we're crazy brave in coming here or just crazy. It's possible we're the kind of beings so courageous we'd board a rocket not knowing if it could survive space. Perhaps there is no making sense of it all from within the game. A satisfactory reason (for extreme suffering) may elude me but this guidance comes through: We exist in a responsive Universe (not an indifferent one) and our Light is here for us.

Friends on the Other Side

Our Light is a point of consciousness the creative medium responds to, but our Story-self was not powered up just to be powered down. This message comes up repeatedly in my communications, in every energy field. My story is not an unfortunate aspect of the game, but a fundamental one. The story is the game. When I gift myself friends on the other side, support grows exponentially. This invisible backing hasn't moved me to the shallow end of deep experiences. It hasn't attempted a rescue mission (to get me the hell out of here) or erased a story I wanted to write.

It does encourage me to be more conscious in my creation, to go at things from unexpected angles, and always remember rule number one - calm down. My unseen friends travel the road beside me and provide company along the way. They never bump me from the driver's seat because I don't want them to. When I ask for assistance, I pay close attention to what shows up. The energy of things is paramount in this relationship because my ego filters what comes through. Fear means specifics aren't my guidance of choice, generalities are. I am not seeking God-given directives but help understanding how I might get where I'd like to go.

One morning I'd finished writing and headed to town to buy groceries and run a few errands. Several unusual items were on my list and one after another, I found them. Support was rampant and my day was going so well it bordered on being ridiculous. I found myself offering up a heartfelt thank you to my friends on the other side. But in expressing this gratitude, I immediately felt to question it. What exactly was I appreciating here?

When you are taught to believe in a God who answers yes to some prayers and no to others (and you're not privy to the why) the unseen is hard to trust. It's like being a pawn in a game where an unknowable entity is playing you and keeping you in the dark. Not pleasant. Few things have changed my perception more than deciding I don't exist to deal with reality – reality exists to respond to me.

The core of what I choose to believe about unseen support can be summarized this way: my Light understands and wants for me, what I want for me. This does not mean conditions and circumstances are always favorable, but that my Inner Being is focused on the substance of my desires and the creative medium responds affirmatively. The good I'm asking for is always given. How things unfold in any particular telling of our tale, reflects complicated energy patterns at play. Patterns to allow. But in the interest of expanding support know this - thank you is not a helpful response when it carries an underlying message that someone outside of us is the bestower of our wellbeing, as it puts us in a supplicating position. *Please give me the good I desire* is not the same as *help me to be a receiving channel to the good I am asking for; help me align with this yes.*

My thanks, then, is not to an authoritative God who generously grants my requests but to a God Force living through me, as me. I am not being played. I am the player and the entire game is responding to me, all aspects of me, both seen and unseen. I offer thanks to my friends on the other side for opening my heart to love in this world; for showing me my life has value, for never leaving me alone. I'm grateful for their encouragement and understanding (not patience) when I come to them with the same struggles over and over again. When I align with support, reality takes on a depth and dimension lacking without it. Having friends in the unseen world is significant for to know the Light is backing us, is to shift the entire spectrum of the game.

The Rest of the Story

My failure to tell you much about my ridiculously good day was a bit of a tease and I dislike that when I'm reading a book. I want the author to bring me into their story, sharing specifics so I can relate to them as a real person living a real life. I think I avoided doing so because at times the Law of Attraction strikes me as frivolous, (the whole *think about a car and the Universe will bring you one* kind of scenario) and this good day was all small stuff. I have hard days. Moments when discouraged energy knocks me down and I wallow there. Times when support in my life feels most like a hug to carry me through. But the small stuff is not without meaning. Support assists us in ways both big and small. Details are not trifling, but part of our day-to-day story. When I'm able to align with encouraging energy, I find myself in a reality so accommodating, I'm elated to be here. This was one of *those* days!

As I mentioned before, I'd spent the morning writing about support. Pleased with what I'd accomplished, I saved my work and turned my attention to the day ahead. We had family coming for a weekend visit and the big news was the upcoming birth of our granddaughter – so exciting! I had a list of things I needed for meals plus some odd items I was hoping to find.

As I headed out of my little town to the bigger town where we shop, a yard sale sign caught my eye. The family had a nice crib and a small dresser for sale - $10 each. Sold! I loaded them up and hit the road again. My next stop was a favorite thrift store, where I scored bumper pads for the crib in like-new condition and an unopened wood-crafting sign I could paint for our playhouse remodel. (We'd decided to name it *The Hummingbird House* in honor of our tiny new arrival entering the game!)

At the main grocery store, I hit a couple of snags. They had no pepitas (which are green pumpkin seeds) I needed for a chocolate bark recipe. They did have brioche buns in an expensive 8-pack at the bakery. I passed, hoping Costco might have them for a lower price. At first, it appeared Costco had neither item, as I'd checked in all the usual places with no success. Disappointed, I realized I was going to have to do something I didn't want to do – drive to another store. This juncture, this point in the story, is important. I let go of perfection and held on to support. *Not perfect – not a problem – still supported.*

As I entered the check-out line, I remembered something we needed from the freezer section and began making my way to the back of the store. This led me past a free-standing shelf of brioche buns (12 pack, low price) followed by a display of mixed pepitas, dried cranberries, and sunflower seeds. Placing this last item in my cart, I considered how the berries and seeds would be a great addition to the bark and lightheartedly told the Universe it was showing off! I haven't even mentioned the beautiful weather, delicious lunch and nice people I'd encountered. This is what happens when I'm living in the energy of support – things go better than I hope and I feel loved in personal, practical ways.

Small stuff is big stuff when it hammers home the point reality wants to help us. I've learned to accept whatever shows up (*not perfect – not a problem – still supported*) and be a bit loosey-goosey with my expectations, for in my experience this mindset better aligns me with support. Life has my back. At times I'm in an energetic place where damn if things aren't going well for me. At other times, I hold to my knowing that love is with me on this journey, unfailingly assuring me where I am is okay and who I am is enough.

Trust

Have you ever asked your Light for help and felt there was no response? I have and the ensuing doubts threw a wrench in my ability to align with support. How do you trust something you can't count on? You don't. Confidence here is a must-have, so getting to the bottom of this dilemma was huge (not huge hard but huge significant) and I'm eager to share with you what I discovered. Turns out there is no radio silence, but there are spotty connections. Our human tendency toward confirmation bias (interpretations that confirm what we already believe) is hindering. Fortunately, our Light works around this.

At times the thing we're asking for causes the interference because it is specific. We think we know precisely what we need and shut down other possibilities. We tell the Universe *I want A which must come to me through B* and the Universe knows *B won't bring us A*. They're presenting option C and we're ignoring it. What happens then? Guidance in the form of roadblocks and radio static.

When I decided to open an alterations business, I began gathering equipment I would need. I owned a good sewing machine and had purchased a backup model, but there were issues with my serger (an overlock contraption to cut and finish fabric edges.) Constantly breaking plates and in the shop for repairs, it needed replacing. But as it cost me $2500, I decided to make due. Further complicating matters, I'd inadvertently given its power cord to a yard sale customer. He'd stopped by my house a few weeks later to get the right cord for the machine he'd purchased, but I wasn't home and my teenagers didn't ask for a name or any contact information. With no idea how to reach him, I asked Life to support me by putting us in touch and then I would visualize this happy outcome.

Weeks went by and nothing happened. No phone call, no chance meeting, no second visit. I asked again. I visualized. I aligned with a good outcome. Zilch, zip, nada. Frustrated, I couldn't wait any longer and bought a used power cord. Arriving home, I plugged it in and it didn't work! The whole situation had turned into one big hassle and when the sewing center offered to sell me a brand-new cord for $200, I wasn't feeling much support. I did not want to pay that much money to keep a substandard machine operating. Irritated, I began checking out inexpensive sergers online. I ended up buying a low-price model for $300, thinking it would get me by until I had funds for a better one. But it sewed like a dream. It cut easily, the stitching was perfect and I was so glad I bought it.

A few months later, I ran into a friend from a gardening class I'd taken. Turns out her husband was the one who had purchased my sewing machine and we exchanged power cords. Now I know the Universe could have arranged for us to meet up sooner but then I would have kept my old machine. If the used power cord I'd purchased had worked, I would have kept my old machine. If a new cord had been less expensive, I would have kept my old machine.

The fact I was hitting roadblocks here was not evidence of a lack of support but guidance from an intelligence with more information than me. Life knew what I needed was not a cord for my crappy serger but an inexpensive, better-working serger altogether. Experiences like this have changed the way I view support. When things are not unfolding easily, I step back and re-evaluate. I can't know for certain the specifics that will take me where I'd like to go but my Light does. Understanding this means I'm more open to possibilities and less prone to pushing agendas.

What happens if we don't step back, but power through, clinging to specifics that lead away from our desire? No big deal. Life doesn't say, *well she chose poorly and there's nothing to be done about it now* or throw up its hands and decide to go help someone who's listening. Our Light is constant and caring. In fact, if a communication coming through seems irritated or harsh in any way, I know it's not my Light I've tapped into, but my ego. Our stories are supported but get in the way at times. Trust Life doesn't have a problem with our humanness and will meet us where we are.

Vast and Unshakeable

The examples I've shared to this point reflect support at the shallow ends of the ocean. Help along the beach as we walk a few inches in the water. But what happens when we take a step into the sea and the bottom drops out from under us? When the wind begins to howl and towering waves crash over us? When an undertow pulls us into danger and the shore gets further and further from sight? What about the energy of support then?

While studying to be a teacher, a personality assessment was given in one of my courses. While explaining the categories, the professor stated scoring over a certain percentage on the empathy scale, put us at risk of engaging in inappropriate relationships with our students. Skeptical, my high score concerned me not at all. In my opinion, if you didn't care deeply for your students what was the point in being a teacher? Nothing like the over-confidence of the inexperienced. My first job was at a regular high school and I loved it. I remember thinking I'd do this work even if I didn't get paid, that's how rewarding it was. And healthy boundaries were a non-issue. But then I took a position at an Alternative high school where the students enrolled had challenging life circumstances. Many were teen parents, former drop-outs, or struggled with substance abuse, legal troubles, and home issues. These kids needed connection and I was all in. When told the students saw me as one of them, I took it as a compliment but in truth, it was a red flag.

Being married, having an affair of any kind went against my moral code and involvement with a student was unthinkable. So developing a friendship with a young man I was attracted to did not concern me like it should have. By the time I recognized the danger, I'd already made the choices (going there in my mind) that put me where I ended up. Hurting so many people. Accountability is not negated by understanding the mental gymnastics we use to engage in behavior both unethical and immoral. It does empower us to step on and stay on a path of integrity. To see clearly how we lit the fuse that blew up a bomb as well as the fallout from the explosion, is to stand in a changed place and live a better life. But these insights were years in coming and apply more to other energy fields.

Friend, I am sharing this part of my story with you because the bomb I blew up revealed a level of support unknown to me before. The legal system is slow moving and even if you plead guilty, there is a great deal of time between being arrested and knowing the outcome. I spent one night in jail and eleven months in legal limbo, worrying I might go to prison and what this would mean for my husband and young children. Eventually, I was sentenced to three years of probation. Before this resolution, however, the presence of an unseen world became evident and the support if offered vast and unshakeable. When I would lay down to sleep a blanket of peace and protection would descend upon me unlike anything I have experienced before or since. Moments of panic would arise and this calming influence would slow my racing heart and help me breathe again.

People sent cards and letters, offering money and sharing mistakes they'd made so I'd feel less alone. A woman I'd never met, showed up on my doorstep with a lovely plant for my garden. The kind and caring principal I worked with, invited students to write letters on my behalf and gave me copies. One young man wrote, "It was so hard for me to come to this country and try to learn English. Mrs. Merrick's words of encouragement stayed with me and helped me believe in myself. I always think about what she said when things get hard." His words stayed with me and helped me to forgive myself over the years for not being the kind of teacher I wanted to be.

What I learned about the energy of support is this: *rock bottom creates an opening because when you can't help yourself - you let Life step in.* It's good to feel strong, capable and empowered but there is a force in existence that moves mountains when we surrender to it. The first step in a twelve-step program is acknowledging we are powerless over our addiction and the second step is believing a power greater than ourself can restore us to sanity. This power, greater than myself, was there for me over and over again. The snapdragons in my front flowerbeds grew to be three feet tall and I knew they were a blessing from a world which loved me. My future was completely up in the air and I'd never felt more protected. I knew whatever happened, things would be alright. There was no saving myself and so I let Life save me.

I don't recommend running your life train off its tracks to reveal how supported you are, but few of us complete this journey without a serious challenge or two. The point is – if we find ourselves traversing hell, there is a heaven who wants to help us. It was absolutely to my benefit I had no one to blame for my troubles but myself. If someone had wronged me (or it seemed Life had wronged me,) it's likely I would have gotten caught up in being a victim. Fear, anger and resentment would have held more of my attention. Because this was all on me, I was more accepting than resisting. **Two key lessons learned:** first, surrender and support are positively correlated, meaning they move in the same direction. When one goes up, so does the other. Second, at no point was I vilified or condemned by All that Is. There was never a glib *it matters not who you've hurt* response or here is *a free pass to avoid all consequences* but a deep admonition I was still worthy of love, in spite of everything.

More Thoughts on Support

Show Me the Money

Support is **the** energy which attracts money. I've found it to be far more useful than abundance in this regard. A full cup euphoria, abundance is a celebratory energy that lives in an elevated place. Support fills our cup in the first place and as an assisting energy, it has no fixed vibrational range. It will meet us at our highest highs and lowest lows, thus fulfilling its purpose.

Money is a medium through which Life supports us and we support each other. We can't eat it, but it lets us purchase food. We can't live in it, but it allows us to have a home. We can't drive it, but it pays for transportation. Money can't buy the best feelings here (like love) but it does play a significant role in their expression.

If you're like me, hardly a day goes by you don't spend money. Funds leave our hands constantly. We might be excited if we are purchasing something we want; resentful if we believe an item is overpriced; fearful if we aren't certain we have enough to meet our needs. We may be worried if we lack confidence in a purchase; happy to donate to a cause we believe in; irritated if we think of grocery shopping as an unpleasant chore to be completed. How we feel is a direct result of the story we choose and the meanings we assign. We can opt in to support by deliberately adding context that puts us in a different mindset. Consider this belief: *Every time I spend money, I am supporting the life of another.* Every single time? Yes. This foundational shift in perception moves energy.

Begin by noticing even if you have limited means, those means support the lives of many people. Consider the purchase of dog food. When you buy it, you are supporting those who came up with the recipe and the farmers who raised or grew the ingredients. You are supporting those who designed the logo, who manufactured the product and put together its packaging. Support is being given to those who transport the dog food and to those who sell it. And of course, you and your dog benefit (he gets to eat and you get to care for him!) It could be argued I'm making this transaction bigger than it is. After all, the financial benefit here has to be far less than a dollar in every direction. But such logic misses the mark. Is there a single individual buying thousands of pounds of dog food each week and supporting everyone? No, there is not. You are providing support, even if you are only one of a million buying this product. Support has little to do with a dollar amount and everything to do with our connection to Life.

The money is going anyway, so why not let it serve us? Why not tie spending to support and turn a financial subtraction into an energetic addition? When I log in to pay bills, I consider how convenient it is our garbage is collected each week. I picture the woman I wave to who does this job and I opt in. When I schedule a payment to Les Schwab, I appreciate the tires we bought and a company of topnotch people who provide great service and I opt in. When I write out a check to my mom to pay our share for the family cabin, I think about those who fill the propane tank, who plow the driveway of snow, who created technology alerting us to falling temperatures, who offer insurance should the cabin burn to the ground.

I opt in and feel differently. It isn't just that what goes around, comes around and so I'm attracting money because of this attitude. It's that my participation in the supportive circle of Life places me firmly in a kinder, more abundant reality.

Show Me a Way

I am not a fan of capitalism. I could go on a rant and detail how corporate America is wrecking our country (one segment of society at a time) with their greed and I would not be wrong. But being right isn't that helpful in my world. I want to allow more than resist; to clear my vision not cloud it; to feel more supported than thwarted and I can't have these things when I'm angry the world isn't as I think it should be.

Support is a navigating energy that shows me a way. Last night I told my husband I had a headache in my eye after dealing with the company who provides us with television service. Frustrated over a plan change they seem incapable of implementing, time spent checking out their competitors left me fantasizing about homesteading in Alaska. Irked, I can't decide if we should stay with their overpriced (but easier to use) service or switch to a more reasonably priced, online option.

Lately everywhere I shop, I'm asked to make a donation. What used to feel like an opportunity to be generous now seems coercive. A corporation recently bought out one of our local thrift stores and the prices have increased dramatically. (Profiting from donated items strikes me as a sham but is another way for big business to make money.) My last visit to this particular store involved overhearing a valid complaint about the higher prices as well as being asked to donate additional money with my purchase. I can afford to make a small donation everywhere I shop but if I feel resentment, it's not the kind of giving I'm interested in.

In the big picture, these are small problems. But nothing we are living is insignificant when it comes to our energy. We all have conditions in life that annoy us; that pull us out of peace and invite drama; that put us in a place of resistance. Knowing support could help me find a way, I got centered and approached these concerns from my deepest understanding of reality and the answers became clear to me. I want to be supportive of the person behind the cash register; of the individual talking to me on the phone. I want their day to be better because of their interaction with me. It's likely they are getting paid low wages by a company unconcerned for their wellbeing and I don't need to add to their troubles by dumping my frustrations on them. Donations will be about the moment at hand and the person in front of me. Television has improved so much in my lifetime. The quality and quantity of shows available is remarkable and I'm going to hold my attention there. One of our high-tech kids may help us make the transition to online viewing (turns out that was easy!) or we may stay with the low-tech option but either choice will be made from acknowledging abundance in my life.

If our choice to align with what we desire summons it into this world then anger directed at big business will do little to correct the imbalance of power in this country. Sowing seeds of support and appreciation, however, will. This assertion is personal for me because I have an inner attorney who wants to prove her case (unfettered capitalism is toxic and should be abolished!) but any path outside of energy alignment is a losing proposition. We can have a revolution, but if better energies aren't in play, we'll merely swap out one exploiter for another.

Road Report: Tipping expectations in the United States have gone off the rails. What used to be standard for a few professions like full-service wait staff or the stylist who cuts your hair, has turned into an ask everywhere. Would you like to leave a tip for the cashier who sold you cheese curds at the dairy store, for the attendant who processed your movie theater ticket, or at the self-serve kiosk (for who knows who?) where you checked in at the airport? Seriously? I don't want to make the person at the car wash feel unappreciated but why, exactly, do I need to tip them? Especially when their job appears to be selling me the monthly plan? Tipping in these situations feels like manipulation because it is. Tips supplement low wages, attracting workers while keeping company profits high. (Big business – always on the take.) Every time we turn around, they have their hands in another pocket and it's exasperating.

We could turn this situation on its head and transmute our anger into vision. What if we started a $1.00 tipping movement? Every time a screen asks, we give a dollar. This specific amount (for non-customary tipping situations) would be an offer of support to the person (or kiosk) in front of us and an energetic vote for the world we want to live in. Friends, I'm convinced we have power here. It's okay to get mad and I'm on board with dissolving one capitalistic enterprise at a time by shifting our financial backing (the government is owned by the rich so who we elect will change nothing). But if anger is dominant, the revolution fails. What's bad must be a launching point for better. Our visionary energy needs somewhere to land, something to build, someone to support. Let's use our Light to stick the landing and change the world.

To Clap and Cheer!

The applause of a single human being is of great consequence.
~ Samuel Johnson

A story is told about a young boy who hoped to participate in the school play. When the day of selections arrived, his mother was concerned he would not get a part and worried how this might affect him. In arriving home, the son ran to his mother and with eyes alight, happily announced he'd been chosen to clap and cheer! What a profound lesson. This wasn't a downcast kid making the best of a bad situation – but an upbeat one, wise to a good thing.

When we hold the faulty belief worthwhile parts are the main ones, such wisdom goes missing. There is tremendous opportunity for joy in supporting the dreams and accomplishments of others. We've all been cast in leading and supporting roles. Wholeheartedly embracing both is a most satisfying way to live. Leads may be limited, but consider the vast number of supporting roles available to us. If you ever feel discouraged (as I do) over rampant negativity and want better stuff to focus on – here's a suggestion. Be a follower. Be a backer. Be a fan. Join the club. Buy the t-shirt. Write a review. Compliment. Celebrate. Appreciate. Turn eagerly in the direction of everything you find applaudable.

It serves us to be fans whenever possible. My husband was invited to join a NASCAR fantasy league. I knew next to nothing about this sport and my interest was exceedingly low. Boredom and ignorance are usually companions, for as I learned more about racing, I was fascinated by the details and eager to choose my own favorite driver/team and cheer them on. (There is a lot more to it than left turns!) Each time Chase Elliott comes close to winning, I can barely breathe from nervous excitement. When he won his first race at Watkins Glenn in New York, I wished I'd been there in person to celebrate with other number 9 fans!

I adore Adam Lambert (thank you American Idol!) Over the years, I've bought his music, traveled to concerts and visualized his success. I feel connected to the other fans (we call ourselves Glamberts) and see our combined support merging into a dynamic, compelling force. One concert in Phoenix found me enthusiastically hugging a stranger, mutually thrilled to be there because - *Adam*! Over-the-top focus elevates our stories, taking us to a higher plane. When we add our energy to the dream of another, it becomes our dream as well.

At times such passion is labeled delusional or escapist. Sports fans, in particular, take flak for personally identifying with teams. Remember the SNL Star Trek skit, where William Shatner tells fans to get a life?! While funny, I believe the criticism here is misguided. If no one felt much fervor in watching the games, listening to music or reading books, would anything special be happening? How thrilling was it to get in line at midnight to purchase the newest Harry Potter book!? (I'm jealous of kids reading these books for the first time.) Who do you suppose is having the better time here? People whose energy is confined to their personal experience or those who choose to be a pulling participant in the expansion of all that is? Support reveals there aren't a few super-talented people in this world while the rest of us must settle for crumbs. There is magic in our connections and when we choose to be a fan of anything, we become an essential part of it.

Life is remarkable and we participate in that together. All day long, we have the chance to clap and cheer for other people and how good it feels to do so. Certain situations lend themselves to actually standing, clapping and cheering but we can be supportive in less direct ways as well. Here in Idaho, the city of Twin Falls has promoted extensive landscaping all over town and I find myself continually complimenting them on a job well done. There is a teacher in my community who every time her name enters my awareness, is offered an energetic high-five for the incredible difference she's made in the lives of so many. I have told her this in person, but I feel to celebrate her accomplishments every time I think about her. (Cheers Diane!) A Facebook friend is super close to her sisters, and when I see their light-hearted, appreciative posts, I admire what they've created and think *way to go*!

Offering applause is a heartening way to live in the energy of support. Unproblematic, it invites us to share the perception Life has of our value. The contrast between approaching others with high regard or tearing them down with criticism is like a feast or a famine; a table of plenty or not enough; a table we set.

Road Report: My oldest daughter is a huge Taylor Swift fan. Over the years she insisted her family be fans too (so we wouldn't miss out). That she strong-armed us into becoming Swifties, became an inside joke. My husband's co-workers give him a hard time for knowing the lyrics to every song. One December, she and I argued because I was listening to Christmas music and not Taylor's new album! After viewing the Eros Tour movie, each one of us felt to thank her for pulling us into something remarkable.

The sensation of Taylor Swift is not singular, but collective and truly, it is something else!

When I fall into negative nitpicking, (leaving me starved for good energy) I say to myself, *Julie, don't be a chicken pecker.* Biology means chickens don't have much choice in their behaviors, but I do. Let me set a better table by offering a shoutout to TikTok - with Jenn, who shares something positive every day and Matt, where the dogs are good each week. (*Please tell your dog I said hi!* is a sentiment close to my heart.) Walking around Home Depot, I find pleasure in being a doer who gets things done! The Idaho Botanical Garden has a new enthusiast member – me! Resident Alien is such a great show – Sahar for president! Clapping and cheering seats me before a banquet and leaves me convinced this human gig is a good one.

When Home is a Hug

Warm, familiar scents drift softly from the oven, and imprint forever upon our hearts that this is home and we are loved.
~ Arlene Stafford Wilson

The energy of support is deeply embedded in the concept of home. To say something or someone *feels like home* is to offer a real compliment. Can we generate a hug to live in? With vibrations so supportive, we're bolstered merely entering the space?

Domesticity gets a bad rap that is not undeserved. Historically, women were confined to the role of homemaker, which tied such work to gender inequalities. When they entered the workforce, the division of labor did not shift accordingly. The issue isn't so much the caring of our homes but the parasitical nature of many male/female relationships. When one partner habitually relies on or exploits the other and gives little in return, it's a leeching situation. That many women are opting out of such relationships makes sense and is advisable. In Australia, native women were treated like pack animals. Changing one's culture may require ditching the load and walking away.

Such concerns, while meaningful, are a diversion here. Let's set them aside (for now) and delve into this truth: we all live somewhere. And that somewhere is an untapped resource for support.

I once attended a garden tour where some yards had been professionally landscaped while others were brought into being through years of hard work and passion. The difference was striking. The first group was pleasing and the second soulful. Our homes work the same way. The level of support they offer is proportional to the level of ourselves we've put into them. This doesn't mean we must do all the work alone or purchase the best of everything. It means if we want our homes to feel like a hug, we must touch them with our essence. They must reflect us in meaningful ways and benefit from care we give them. The creation of a supportive environment is an inside job. It isn't just showing up to a place where someone else has cooked dinner and done the laundry. If we are not a participating entity (both giving and receiving), the benefit is minimal.

I find it helpful to imagine myself holding an energy stamp that determines the nature of my environment. Am I marking *resentment* when I wash the dishes? *Impatience* when I vacuum out the car? *Irritation* over having at least a thousand apples to pick up before I mow the yard? *Overwhelmed* when I note how much there is to do? Happily working from sunup to sundown is not the hug I'm envisioning here (and a heavy pruning for our fruit trees is happening this spring), but seeing my approach more clearly is. I want to feel *bountiful* when I prepare a meal, stock the pantry, and put clean dishes away. *Comforted* when I hear the furnace kick on, fold towels warm from the dryer, or quietly stand by a window and watch the rain fall. *Cheerful* when I lift Christmas ornaments from their storage box. *Content* when I make my bed each morning and tuck into the covers at night. I also find it helpful to ask myself, if a visitor came to my home, how much soul would greet them? Would they know for certain they'd entered a space that truly mattered to the people who live here?

Support is about ownership. It is a switch from merely inhabiting spaces to creating them. When I drive around my community, what do I feel? If I've put nothing of myself into the town where I live, probably not much. I wonder at times if the rampant desire to escape reality doesn't reflect the choice to put so little of ourselves into reality. Support turns apathy to attention; neutrality to involvement; disassociation to deep connection.

The staff at the small alternative high school where I taught worked with our students to create a home-like environment. We didn't have a teacher's lounge but a school lounge where everyone gathered for lunch. Once a week, we'd bake bread to share with plenty of butter and honey (frozen loaves that were easy to pop in the oven and smelled amazing!) Weekly cleaning and holiday decorating were part of our schedule. Improvement projects like planting flowers out front and painting a mural made the space feel like ours and that we'd made it better. Bulletin boards showcased the interests and accomplishments of every student. Classes were a safe place and this was non-negotiable. No mean humor allowed. Instilling a sense of belonging and ownership was a primary goal achieved. The only downside was a few students may have delayed graduating because they didn't want to leave us. Perhaps they needed a home more than a diploma right then.

An Anchor and an Advocate

Support is sitting down to a steaming bowl of soup on a chilly winter evening. It is the reassuring pressure of a safety bar as the ride begins to move. It is the sound of a loved one's voice. Support is soothing like lip balm. Warming like morning sun. Stable like well-made furniture. It is oxygen in the air we breathe, money in our bank account, a clean bill of health. A light left on for us, support is an anchor and an advocate; patronage and protection; wings and a place to land.

Corgis are popular in Yellowstone Park. When we had our sweet boy, Bentley, people would walk across parking lots to meet him. This always made me happy and now I do the same. Last summer while enjoying views from a lodge balcony, I noticed a woman walking a beautiful corgi below. I hightailed my way down to meet them and the woman was super friendly. She told me after a recent vet visit, she was reminded her time with her sweet girl was limited. And then she said to me, "We're here because I want to show her the world." I think about this encounter when I think about support. My Light wants to show me the world. She can't gift me with a pain-free story that lasts forever but she will buy me treats and give me ear scratches and make a comfortable bed for me to sleep on. She will help me live my best life and love me with all of her heart through the end of my journey.

Friend, every step we take along this wild and crazy path is an opportunity to invite an energy that has our back, gives a damn, knows us intimately and loves our humanness. We are never alone and we are not unknown.

FOUR

The Energy of Appreciation

Appreciation is the magic formula you've been seeking.
~ Abraham

Appreciation is a magic formula because <u>it isn't asking for change.</u> It's not waiting around for improved weather, a bonus check, or a vacation day. It isn't attached to a rewarding job, time with family, or even a restful night's sleep. It doesn't need to be fit or in love or on the brink of some exciting accomplishment. Appreciation isn't holding out for a satisfactory story but honing in on what is pleasing about the story at hand.

What a relief it's been to realize I don't need to go shopping for a better life, as appreciation reveals that what I have is enough. More than enough. Influenced to chuck all complaints (petty and valid), I'm moved to give my attention to shade trees, ripe strawberries, and the tremendous good fortune of having a family of eagles to observe. (Two growing babies, a nest perched near the top of a towering, long-dead Douglas fir tree, and a mere ten-minute hike from our family cabin.)

Appreciation is a magic formula because <u>it requires so little effort.</u> The less work it feels to be, the closer our alignment. Appreciation will often lead us into transcendent energies like rapture, connection, and bliss but it is none of these things. It is not a treasure to hunt down and protect or solve clues to find. Appreciation doesn't ask us to go big but go. Easily. Comfortably.

My life is far from perfect, but quite close to wonderful and appreciation highlights this perception. The inspirational writer/speaker Steve Maraboli said, *"The more I understand the mind and the human experience, the more I begin to suspect there is no such thing as unhappiness; there is only ungratefulness."* A straightforward path to a more generous, kind-hearted life is beneath our feet. No gate to unlock, map to navigate, or trail to blaze but a simple choice to welcome all that is agreeable as we move along our way.

A Thousand, Thousand Reasons

One of the greatest gifts this transient reality offers is expanding our capacity to cherish Life. The title of one of my favorite books is *Gilead*, written by Marilynne Robinson. The principal character, John Ames, is a Christian minister who spends his life contemplating the mysteries of our human existence. Repeatedly his considerations give me pause. That to bless is not to enhance but acknowledge sacredness; that setting things apart allows us to perceive their holiness; that many are the uses of adversity. Perhaps experience has no fixed or certain nature, he wondered, and the limitations of our faculties impede our understanding of reality.

One insight, in particular, belongs here and it is this: *There are a thousand, thousand reasons to live this life, every one of them sufficient.* This sentiment burns straight to my soul and answers the question **why**. Why enter a reality where so much pain exists?

When I consider a thousand, thousand reasons, one at a time, and feel their completeness, appreciation and connection merge. Transcendent, I know I am here to look into the eyes of the raccoon who has climbed into my pear tree and it is enough. I am here to visit with a sweet granddaughter as she shares how the lion she's supporting has traveled a lot and it is enough. I am here to lose myself in the sound of cellos as the Airborne Toxic Event performs with the San Francisco Symphony and it is enough.

When I email a compliment to the manager of one of the most inviting stores I've ever set foot in (Raley's on Marconi Street in Sacramento), eat apple slices with chunky peanut butter, or soak in a hot springs pool along the bank of the Colorado river, I don't question why, I know why. When I connect with another being through a shared smile, a hug, or a laugh the sufficiency of any reason stands alone and moves me to cherish Life in the energy of appreciation.

What Matters Most

One criticism leveled against believers in the Law of Attraction is a tendency to bypass negativity, ignoring what we don't want to see. I'll concede this point as I have first-hand experience with it. Repression is a mistake easily fallen into when you understand that where your attention goes, your life follows. But here is another truth to assimilate: appreciation does not proclaim there is *only good*, but that *what is good* matters most.

We don't have to reject the hard stuff but see clearly it isn't the only stuff and it isn't the most important stuff. This is not to make light of difficult things or adopt the somewhat callous claim *it's all good*. Yes, suffering gives us experience and compassion and is often fodder for what we create here. But not always.

That being said, I firmly believe what is good is what matters most. Appreciation is not pretense but revelation, showing us the Astonishing Light of our beings is more important than our shortcomings. That the connection underlying all Life is vastly more significant than the separation we encounter here. That the miracle of existence is of far greater value than the challenges such existence brings into being. There is love and beauty here that eclipses pain.

Stop and Stay (or come back around)

In the interest of feeling better, there are times when we acknowledge things could be worse or deliberately catalog problems we don't have. But bouncing one condition off a worse one is a feeble use of a powerful energy. Uncomplicated appreciation means there are no ramp-it-up shenanigans of any kind. That's why it's easy. Gratitude and thankfulness are helpful for the most part but tend to play off the avoidance or release of suffering. Intense but tainted, they don't offer the clean, clear point of attraction appreciation does.

To illustrate, thankfulness for a meal might come with acknowledging we could be hungry or have less than we do. Gratitude for the presence of family may accompany the realization we could lose them at any time. Heartfelt thanks for surviving an accident carries an acute awareness of what might have happened but didn't. Gratitude and thankfulness are appropriate energies for much of our life experience. It makes sense to be glad for improved health after an illness, sunshine after days of rain, money after a struggle to make ends meet. But my explorations have taught me a most important lesson - stand-alone appreciation is a vastly more compelling, life-altering energy. One telltale component sets it apart: indifference to contrast. Appreciation doesn't care. It asks no troublesome questions like where did this positive thing come from? Did I earn it? Do I deserve it? Will it stick around?

Appreciation lands on what pleases, stopping and staying there. This chair is comfy. This show is hilarious. This color is soothing. This bread is delicious. My thoughts frequently take twisty turns like this:

Wow, what a lovely spring day (*I better enjoy it because a pancake on a hot griddle summer will be here soon!*)

How pleasant it is to drive in Twin Falls early on a weekend morning (*this town is growing so fast and the increased traffic stresses me!*)

What a treat it is to have dinner out (*I'm kind of over the whole cooking every day for the rest of my life thing!*)

Did you notice how all my contrasting thoughts have exclamation points?! It's not that I have some big issue with bitching, I don't. Complaints often add humor, making our conversations more colorful and our humanness more relatable. But in its most effective form, appreciation is without resistance. It doesn't summon what we like and immediately compare it to what we don't. It begins and ends with the good stuff. It isn't that this energy wears blinders or is oblivious to what is happening. *It doesn't care.* The exclamation point comes after the first observation, not the second. And that's the only move we need to make.

So *quitcherbitchin'* may help us reign in a bad attitude but the facts are we have hot summers, traffic is terrible at times and cooking dinner every night gets old. It helps to imagine appreciation like a balloon and if I want it to soar, I must cut it free from the contrast holding it down. Not because what I don't like is unmentionable, but because it's tethering and I'm going for flight here. Note what gladdens you. <u>Stop and stay.</u> And if you fail to stay, just come back around.

How sweet it is to have bats at our cabin! (*Go a quarter mile up the hill and the mosquitoes will eat you alive.*) I like these little nocturnal guys – each one eats thousands of bugs every night!

The desert is so peaceful, I love my morning walks! (*And no one is shooting right now - remember the bullet buzzing right by my head?*) Most people are careful, and that experience did provide an interesting story!

What a great year the Sacramento Kings are having! Light the Beam! (*Damn it, I hate the Golden State Warriors. It looks like they're going to win the playoff series and I'm out if that happens.*) Alright – this is a tough one to come back around from. But I'm happy for this California team I've embraced. They haven't been successful in a long time. The coach and players are exceptional, the fans super excited, and I celebrate every time they win and light their giant purple laser!

Contrast isn't my enemy but I refuse to give it top billing; to let it matter more. When I notice what is agreeable and stop and stay (or come back around), I align with the best reality has to offer. There are lakes in Idaho so clear, they mirror the sky above them. The mud at their bottom is not stirred up but settled. The energy of appreciation is pristine lakes and soaring balloons; unpolluted buoyancy and resilience of spirit.

A Lord and Savior

I like basketball. More specifically, I like Spurs basketball. I may be a native Idahoan, but this Texas team has given me a slew of reasons to be a fan. Foremost, Tim Duncan, whose humility and excellence are unparalleled. Then there is Coach Pop and his terse interviews. The players are loyal, selfless, and comprise an all-star cast rather than one star with a supporting cast. I like their passing game, their intact identity, and how they recruit players from all over the world. Last year I bought an NBA League pass, watched every game, and understood why the players are exhausted when the playoffs roll around. NBA Basketball is a huge plus in my life.

However, in the past couple of years, the Golden State Warriors have become annoyingly dominant. When one team ends up with all the best players, it takes all the fun out of the sport. If Kevin Durant had chosen to play with the Spurs, I would have struggled to continue being a fan of what I consider 'my' team. But this is me focusing on a problem instead of what is pleasing. My son-in-law shared that his best friend is a Warriors fan who describes Stephen Curry as Our Lord and Savior. That's funny and makes me question my serious attitude. I quit watching basketball back when the Los Angeles Lakers were running roughshod over everyone (and missed three Spurs Championships!) because I let what I didn't like matter more to me than what did.

Humor can reframe our perceptions. After all, we Spurs have our own Lord and Savior, Kawhi Leonard and assuming he doesn't jump ship on us and become a Laker, our future looks bright. I prefer talent being spread around, so all the teams have a fighting chance, but I will not bail on basketball if that doesn't happen. Rigid expectations are tricksters, leading me away from and not toward what I want. Should the Spurs rise again, I will be around to cheer them on.

Writing about basketball quickly becomes old news. Kawhi Leonard did leave and the Spurs are rebuilding. I've learned to appreciate a number of teams (Go Raptors! Go Bucks! Go Kings!) and give myself permission to check out when the Warriors take over. I don't enjoy watching them win (or hearing the commentators drool over their championship DNA) and there is no reason to do so. Appreciation is not a push to like what we don't but elevate what we do.

The Glue that Makes Things Stick

What if you woke up one morning and discovered a life comprised exclusively of things you felt appreciation for yesterday? Would an abundant world greet you, or would your surroundings be relatively sparse? Would there be clouds moving across the sky? Wind rushing through the trees? The tang of citrus as you peeled an orange? Would there be funds in your checking account, a working car in your garage, and a furnace to heat your home? Would your community still have a grocery store, a park, and a library? Would there be roast chicken and veggies for dinner, dishes to eat on, and a sink for cleaning up? Would you have a comfortable bed to sleep in, socks and sweaters to wear, and hands to assist you in countless ways? If the only people who stuck around were the ones you felt appreciation for yesterday, how populated would your world be? If apathy created an obvious void, attentiveness would rule the day.

I'm confident I would still hear trains whistling, see frost on the morning grass, and savor my morning coffee. There'd be slip on shoes in the closet, reading glasses in the junk drawer, and a tall tumbler to keep my water icy cold. Our corgi would be around for his belly rubs and our fat cat Morty would lazily nap in the sunshine. I'd still have a husband to go fishing with and curl up to at night, get to visit with my kids most every day, and be planning my garden for the upcoming season. However, my job might go missing, as well as our main bathroom which needs a thorough cleaning. I imagine myself confusedly asking, "Where is my sewing machine, and didn't we have a dining room table?"

If appreciation was the glue that made things stick, I'd squeeze it everywhere. Not because a daily inventory must be completed but because awareness of being part of a wonderful world exists on a continuum. Indifference hampers connection, putting us on the paltry end of a more or less abundant life scale. We are creative beings, whether we see this clearly or not. Our approach matters, so when I notice what often goes unnoticed, the good surrounding me stands out and sticks around.

Low Expectations

In the documentary *Happy*, a Danish man was queried about why people in his country are happier than most. He believed it was the result of their exceptionally low expectations. After laughing over his response, I found myself wondering, could this be true? An expectation is a strong hope for or belief in a particular outcome, usually positive. Unmet expectations identify as a primary cause of divorce. We enter relationships with assumptions of how they will be, and if our partnership doesn't align, we want out. The whole fairy tale wedding thing our culture promotes often strikes me as a set-up for a let-down. Happily-ever-after is a Disney fantasy where the story ends after the rings are exchanged and the couple kisses.

We hold expectations for everything. I had this idea of what it would be like to own a dog, and when we got our Corgi, Bentley, the love and companionship I envisioned are spot-on. But he is not good with toddlers. He doesn't like them, and this is a nerve-wracking mismatch to the *I just met you and I love you* Golden Retriever type personality I'd anticipated.

I recall taking my teenage kids to see the movie *The Last Airbender*. Huge fans of the television series, their disappointment in the film was epic. To this day, its mere mention brings up a heated discussion of how wrong it was in every possible way. I've learned to jokingly abandon all hope before viewing a movie I'm eager to see and if it's a film adaptation of a beloved book, this step is imperative. It occurs to me I need to reality check my excitement for the conclusion of the *Game of Thrones* series. Right now, it is so high, disappointment is inevitable. Jon may never ride a dragon and I need to make peace with that. I'm going to tone down the hype, appreciate how outstanding the show has been, and not believe the last season will be the pinnacle of all television, ever. (Update. Wow, had I scraped dregs from the bottom of the barrel, I could not have lowered my expectations enough to counteract my disappointment in the final season. Much like *The Last Airbender*, it was wrong in every possible way!)

Truthfully, expectations baffle me a bit. Lowering them doesn't mesh with my understanding of the Law of Attraction. How could the choice of expecting life to be disappointing and then being pleasantly surprised when it isn't, be a sound one? Shouldn't we look forward to positive things and so attract them into our experience? The creators of the Game of Thrones series exceeded my expectations spectacularly until the end. At that point, they dropped the ball, and I had nothing to do with it.

The more I consider my experiences and mull them over, the more expectations look like conditions I'm imposing on life. Unexamined requirements; judgments I make in advance. Not appreciative but inflexible, demanding perfection and running interference with energies that allow for the humanness of my experience. Sometimes we drop the ball, all of us.

One reunion weekend I organized a Johnson Family Survivor party. We had buffs for each team, hidden idols, challenges, and a prize for the Ultimate Family Survivor. I have a history of planning fun get-togethers, so I thought we'd have a great time. What I didn't have was any belief all would go off without a hitch. Which was good, because on a hike the evening before the big day, I had an allergic reaction to some wildflowers. I was mostly recovered by morning, but definitely tired and not feeling my best. Reasonable expectations kept me from bemoaning a bit of bad luck and still enjoy myself. One most appreciated memory was watching my nephew carrying out a cube of butter (one of five luxury items his tribe gathered from inside the cabin) and noting how perfectly this reflected the Johnson family priorities!

Lowering our expectations is a bit tongue-in-cheek and certainly not intended to invite a cloud of doom over our heads. But leaning in that direction means we're less inclined to get hung up over idyllic scenarios we think we're due but unlikely to have.

Let Your Pile of Good Things Grow

So what if, instead of thinking about solving your whole life,
you just think about adding additional good things, one at a time?
Just let your pile of good things grow.
~ Rainbow Rowell

Consciously adding to our pile of good things is one way to live in the energy of appreciation. Perhaps you live in California, where you can buy giant avocados at your local grocery store and roses bloom in February. Maybe you have a grandmother who makes the world's best chili, a swimming hole you visit each summer, or an author whose every book engages you. You might have a passion for old automobiles, never miss an episode of Planet Earth, or truly savor an afternoon's siesta. I find myself in the middle of April, a month blessed with tulips blooming, greening grass, and lambkins running through the fields joyfully leaping into the air.

I want to articulate my pile of good things even as I add to it, one focus at a time. How sweet it is to have a new book to read (to add to the pile of engaging books I've already read). How agreeable to have a dark red daylily to plant (to add to the pile of vibrant lilies that delight me). How enticing to have an unfamiliar area to explore (to add to the pile of inviting places I've come to know). I might purchase a fishing license and revive a hobby I had as a kid, or master a new soup recipe and serve it up in brown ceramic mugs. I could spend time in my garden reading poetry by Mary Oliver.

Like packages around a Christmas tree, I want to open and thrill over giant warm slippers, the best-smelling shampoo, squeaky cheese curds, and new red paint for my storage shed. Unlike packages around a Christmas tree, our pile of good things can't be excessive. This isn't empty materialism but fulfilling appreciation where too much or too little doesn't exist. Ours is the option to build a towering mountain of complimentary energy and build a home where the views are spectacular.

My Pinterest World

If Pinterest was looking for a spokesperson, I'd be interested in the job. Much of what I find online could easily be categorized as both a joy and a time suck, but Pinterest is neither of those things. A website generally used to collect recipes, crafting ideas, and better living tips, I use it as an artistic medium for sparking the energy of appreciation. Uplifting and encouraging, I choose from its many quotes and images to create vision boards that spotlight what I like about living in this world.

I've put together a montage for each season and when I look at or add to them, every satisfying aspect gets my attention. Spring is my favorite season, but my *Summertime!* board pleases me most. Undoubtedly because there are so many inviting things about summer to draw from: kids running through sprinklers, watermelon slices, and daisies in bloom; Independence Day celebrations with flags and fireworks, ice cream cones, and pretty glasses of lemonade. There are hammocks to read in, rivers to float, and cut grass to smell; there are the sounds of outdoor concerts, crickets at night, thunderstorms and children playing outside. Summer means barbeques and baseball games, ripe cherries and campfires, water fights, and amusement parks. It is savoring corn on the cob, sweet garden tomatoes, juicy cantaloupe and iced tea. It is wearing flip-flops, buying flats of purple petunias, and riding bikes in the shade. Summer is blissful, and when I visit this board, I forget I have allergies and don't much care for heat. Indeed, these annoyances seem minor when compared to all the lovely things summer is.

My boards have titles like *I Must Have Flowers, The Secret Garden* and *Corgi Happiness*. They let me enter worlds where *I Love the Rain, All Things are Cozy*, and *I'm On the Water*. Romantic courtyards, old libraries, fur kids, and hobbit houses greet me. Sunshine falls on pastel quilts as pies sit cooling on windowsills in *A Cottage World*. Rustic tubs filled with pink and purple hydrangeas live in *Flower Shop Heaven*, while orange slices and tea cup feeders are at home in *For the Birds*.

My *Scotland* board is a favorite, with its photos of old castles, Scottie dogs, Gaelic terms and tartan maps. There are lads wearing kilts, redheaded lassies, coats of arms, and highland meadows. I imagine exploring the dark streets of Edinburgh, entering a charming pub, and hearing bagpipes played. I marvel over the stone bridge that carried the Harry Potter train, fancy the actor James McAvoy and see their blue and white flags flutter in the wind. When I spend time in my Pinterest world, it occurs to me how little it has to do with wealth. My boards are not about attracting things I don't have, but appreciating the wonders here. They reflect an abundance and richness of spirit which are mine now, no matter my income. A trip to Scotland would be expensive, and I don't know I will ever travel there. But it matters not. This creative focus isn't about someday; it is about knowing my life is better right now because Scotland exists, and I appreciate it.

A Bucketed List

A variation on the original theme of recording things you want to do before you die, a bucketed list catalogs favorable things that have already happened. When I call up memories of a satisfying life well underway, my energy is moved. The 'problem of the day' my mind is likely focused upon, shrinks and my capacity to appreciate expands.

My bucketed list reminds me I was an extra in a movie, held a baby tiger, and can make a seriously delicious cheesecake. I wrote a play that made people laugh, spent a weekend with the sweetest dog on the planet (a black Schnauzer named Sarge), and traveled to Marble, Colorado. I've grown popcorn (which I don't recommend), practiced the Danish art of Hygge (which I do), and suspect I met an alien (or an odd person with a dog who both had *Men-in-Black* vibes). I made a Zelda costume for my grandson and learned a long-time customer of mine was the grammy award-winning singer/songwriter Carole King. I've taught swimming lessons, gone spelunking, raised two pigeons with one of my brothers, and spent an incredible afternoon observing a wolf pack in Yellowstone Park.

I don't limit my bucketed list to big items, like becoming a master gardener or taking a stand-up comedy class. Small things have also been engaging, like tasting honeycomb and having a Bernese Mountain Dog sit on my feet (two of the best minutes of my life!) I planned and worked for some events but not all because a bucketed list is not about goals achieved but becoming mindful of a life worth appreciating. This morning, I came across a photo of a young corgi with raccoon-like facial markings (my daughter-in-law said he looked like an adorable red panda) and my world seems rich because of this. Now and again, I need a pick-me-up, an encouraging reminder my life book is a good read, and a bucketed list effectively offers me that.

What Do You Like About?

I find myself wishing I could return to when my children were young and add something to the mix. Captivated, kids embrace the magic here without reservation. But somewhere along our way to adulthood, our excitement gets watered-down, which saddens me. Had I understood the energy of appreciation then as I do now, I would have taken my children's natural inclinations and made them bigger. Encouraging them to appreciate everything in their world would have been a priority in my parenting responsibilities.

I see it all clearly in my mind. I would have made up a game and called it "What do you like about (fill in the blank)?" and then proceeded to coach them into noticing all the things they enjoyed about their bedroom, their toys, their breakfast, their backyard, their friends, and each other. We would have discussed what they thought was fun about visiting grandparents, swimming at the pool, and watching *The Little Mermaid*. A day would not have passed in which we didn't fully consider the wonder of falling rain, popsicles, chalk art, new shoes, kittens, and bedtime stories. We would have celebrated costumes, train whistles, DW dolls and quail as they hopped through the fence and across our yard. I can almost hear my kids describe the thrill of playing in the mud, riding their bikes across town, and climbing to the top of the tree in our front yard; happily telling me why they were glad to live in a world with Harry Potter, birthdays and trampolines.

If I could go back, every day I would teach my children to focus so much on what they like in the world they would carry this habit forever. I cannot imagine a more beneficial gift a parent could give their child. Too often, the primary lesson we pass on to our children is fear; fear the world isn't safe, they won't measure up, that life will be a struggle. We take the blessing of existence and turn it into a burden. Certainly, this life presents challenges for all of us but this doesn't have to be such a deal breaker. A sense of wonder has no expiration date or label reading *for children only*. There is no mandatory 'growing up' required. At any point we can decide to show up like we just got here and be so engaged with our discoveries, a bathroom break annoys us.

Love and Appreciation

If you love a flower don't pick it up, because if you pick it up it dies and ceases to be what you love. So if you love a flower, let it be. Love is not about possession.
Love is about appreciation.
~ OSHO

Let's talk about love. Human Love. Not transcendent love or universal love but the package kind that shows up here, the one with attachment and identification. When I consider how I love my children, the entanglements are obvious. Laced with fear for their safety and wellbeing, it is not a soft energy. The idea of a life without them levels me, and the possibility of unspeakable loss seems intrinsically tied to the experience of parental love.

117

With romantic love, we are often so identified with our partner, we don't know who we'd be apart from them. Completing and reflecting us, the intense high of such couplings is matched only by the devastating lows that commonly follow.

I joke that when I die, I'll be one of those ghosts so attached and identified with their story (my garden specifically) I refuse to leave. For thirty-plus years, my husband and I have lived in this tiny town (that we do like), but as we approach retirement, there would be some real perks to living in a larger place so moving is seriously on the table. But then I look around my home and garden and see my heart and soul infused into every space. This isn't only a place I live, but a part of everything I am and have been. How can I say a premature goodbye (I'm not dead yet!) or leave it for possible neglect? How can this be someone else's home? How does one separate love and attachment? And is that even what I want to do?

When I first explored this topic years ago, I believed human love should be elevated into something better. But my opinion has expanded a bit. Love and loss go hand in hand in this reality and the only way I can imagine this not being so, is if I distanced myself from the beauty and wonder of my own story and I refuse to do that. It seems an empty, small way to live. I suspect a fully awakened being could love without attachment or identification but I am not such a being and the longer I live the more convinced I become a full awakening was not my intention in coming here. The fog of disconnected sleep is lifting but ultimately, I'm here to live a human life. Not from a safe distance, but up close and personal. Not as a witness but a full-on participant. Not half-heartedly but whole-heartedly.

However, the hits don't have to be so hard. There are directions we can lean to lessen the impact; compelling facets to consider and apply; truths

Life wants us to know. The first is appreciation is a powerful tonic for the whole-hearted. Drinking it doesn't mean I won't walk out into my spring garden, that is putting on such a show, and end up crying because it feels like both a thank you and a goodbye. It means my story is fortified and better able to handle the nature of life here. Another, is appreciation is an energy capable of stopping time. And that is a big deal. A huge deal. Present without projection, the timeline halts. What came before and what comes next is less relevant. Morning sun filtering through leaves. The aroma of brewing coffee. Tiny cherries beginning to grow. Love and appreciation for my garden now. Love and appreciation for my home now. Loss recedes when attention returns to the moment at hand.

Most pivotal, however, is realizing our two perspectives (Story and Light) can merge. We always have the option to invite our Light into our experience and value Her perceptions. She isn't in hiding or playing keep away. And She isn't some mysterious entity we can't communicate with. She is the God we are and when I let go of my fears about that, I stop ignoring Her so much.

I held nothing back in the loving of our sweet corgi, Bentley, nothing. The average lifespan for this type of dog is fourteen years. When he turned seven, I recall thinking my time with him was half over and the sensation was like a stab in the heart. Mourning in advance, it was a bittersweet emotion, sullying my short, precious time with him. But how does one love gently when you know separation is inevitable and not long in coming?

How do you feel about this? I questioned, and my Inner Being answered that Her appreciation is unburdened because the fact it doesn't last (within the game) cannot tarnish the wonder of it all. She also encouraged me to Be Like Bentley and ditch the damn narrative more often. Live in joyful oblivion now, and save the tears for later. Her guidance helped me set loss aside and open to appreciation, which meant I could delight in Bentley's soulful brown eyes, obsession with cheese, eagerness for our daily walks in the desert, and whining affection each time we returned home. I was happy giving him belly rubs, taking him out in our canoe, and observing his ongoing battle with the squirrels. I would laugh when our cat refused to respect Bentley's standoffishness and would leap onto his back, tackling him to the ground (Morty's a big cat), and then laugh some more when he gave Morty this *what-is-wrong-with-you?* look every single time. I'd find myself smiling when bedtime arrived, and all requests to come inside were met with a turned head and the pretense of being unable to hear us. Again, having a dog is a short and precious gift, but in truth what gift isn't these things?

Time is fleeting, and as a human, I will feel both love and loss. Everything in our world is a relationship and if I haven't invested enough of myself into those relationships to be sad over an ending, then I'm not here in the way I want to be. **All in** for this adventure, let me take a hearty drink of appreciation, feel it stop time and sense the unencumbered part of me holding this precious story forever.

A New Way of Seeing

My destination is no longer a place, but a new way of seeing.
~ Marcel Proust

The consciousness of a single individual is no small thing because the energetic essence one chooses to embody impacts the entire interconnected web of being. Gandhi's counsel to be the change you wish to see in the world is significant, as choosing to love and appreciate does <u>not</u> mean one life is transformed but that the entire cosmos shifts. We are each a force to be reckoned with and this truth is of profound consequence and justifies hope.

The widely touted idea that we can improve conditions by vilifying what is wrong is a rationalization, an excuse to condemn. We aren't looking to improve things but feed the false sense of superiority we chase when connection is lacking. Being a critic is a life-wrecking endeavor because the choice to tear down our world is the choice to live in ruins. Friend, I hope this isn't the issue for you it is for me. Not a day goes by that I don't have to look at the hammer in my hand and question what I'm doing with it. Am I building or destroying?

This analogy pushes me toward a new way of seeing, a new way of being. Complimentary energy turns the spotlight of our attention into sunshine advancing Life. Connection leads to compassion where we aren't fighting our human nature but choosing our human focus. During the total solar eclipse of 2017, how quickly the heat of a hot August day cooled and how striking it was to feel (however briefly) the loss of our sun. An experiential shake-up, I saw the world differently than I had before. Step back and observe what contemptuous energy creates, how it poisons the well we drink from. Appreciation may get overlooked as positive thinking fluff, but in actuality, it's an antidote for all that ails us.

FIVE

The Energy of Empowerment

She remembered who she was and the game changed.
~ Lalah Deliah

Empowerment reshapes who we think we are and what we believe is possible. It validates the notion that *we create our own reality*. When I first came across this teaching, its significance caused me to sit up and take notice. It did not strike me as nonsense to discard but as a mystery to solve and sparked my fascination with spirituality. Could this be true (that we are at cause in our own life) and if it was, how does this work? For decades I've considered this proposition from every angle. Early on, I realized creation was more about energy than anything else and I put my focus there. But the diversity of our human paths and the contradictions in our conclusions baffled me. I imagined some higher truth pulling us in and placing us all on the same page - directing humanity toward an intended outcome - an awakening, perhaps, where consensus was not only possible but probable.

What I found instead were theories to upend such thinking.

Empowerment is choosing the parameters. **All of them.** We're making it up. Which doesn't mean it's an uncomplicated process. Influenced by countless biological and environmental factors, our consciousness writes code the creative medium executes. We choose through our energy and Life responds.

Exploration is the purpose of reality. **And we cannot do that wrong.** The parameters we choose are always correct – they can't be otherwise. As points of exploration, all positions are equally valid.

Story Waters offers two radical teachings that serve as effective launching points to empowerment. The first is while we are **not** the most powerful force in **the** Universe, we **are** the most powerful force in **our** Universe. The second is we are not here to discover the nature of reality but create it. Consider for a moment how these ideas make you feel. Do you find them thrilling or terrifying? Or (more likely) a combination of both? Then decide, as the God you are, if you want to move in their direction or not.

Road Report: Before we go any further, clarifications are needed. When I first began this journey, I was over-the-top thrilled about the Law of Attraction. The idea we had influence here seemed the best news ever. While sharing my enthusiasm, a fellow meditation attendee responded how interesting he found it most seekers begin in that place and end up elsewhere. Looking back, I know he meant well, but it felt like he'd told me I was seated at the children's table. He was right, of course. Not that my interests were childish, but that what began simply would gain depth over time.

Friend, I came close to pulling the entire empowerment section from my book. Someone I love deeply was hurting and focus on empowerment left me scrambling for control in the game. Hoping if I could just get myself right – things would be alright.

The biggest danger in the Law of Attraction is its blaming nature. If our life sucks, it's our own doing. And that's supposedly good news, right? Because it means we have power. **Full stop.** Being told we create our own reality can feel like a kick when we're down. Like other people can attract good things and here we are in the worst of places. Maybe we're alone, battling a serious illness, can't find work, have lost someone we love, or have been traumatized by violence. Maybe we can't see a light at the end of our tunnel and the completion of this game would be a blessed relief.

Compassion arises when we understand the complexity of creation. Of course we have influence here, but without the energy of connection, it's a moot point. My approach to empowerment has been more practical than mystical and I did not give the energy of love the weight it deserves. Perhaps we are here to be gentle in a broken game; to embrace a journey that will hit us hard; to gather shards and make what art we can. Story Waters has another teaching I ask you to hold foremost in your awareness before reading on: <u>WHO we will become in loving ourselves is the reason we exist.</u>

Fear

Out of perfection nothing can be made.
~ Joseph Campbell

Empowerment is scary. Hella frightening, in fact. Hit with the knowledge my energy creates moved me from thrilled to terrified pretty damn fast. Because control is hard to come by (and I believed it necessary), so creatorship felt like more responsibility than I wanted or could handle. But I was wrong.

Empowerment stopped being so worrisome when I changed my approach. When I let my Light teach me what I was asking to understand. Allowing is imperative because we will never control our way out of contrast. If I held an article of faith, it would be Joseph Campbell's teaching that out of perfection nothing can be made. This world isn't paradise. It's potential. It's prospects. It's possibilities. And it's exactly how we intended it to be.

A complicated pool of energies, we are not observing reality from the sidelines. We're in it up to our necks and sometimes the water is over our heads. Again allowing, not controlling, is the energy that makes it possible to swim here. When we are pliant, our body relaxes and we float. When we tense up, our body contracts and we sink. After rereading the section on allowing, I realize I'll be repeating here much of what I wrote there. It has to be. These energies (allowing and empowerment) are so enmeshed they unfailingly activate together.

My husband and I watch a lot of nature shows. My heart hurts for the polar bears and their predicament. Couldn't we build floats for them since the ice is gone? I'm not okay with their extinction and yet it is estimated over 99.9% of all species that have ever lived are now extinct. More likely than not, humans will become part of that statistic. The sheer number of us and how we live is unsustainable. Being the most powerful force in MY Universe doesn't mean I can change this. I can't save the polar bears. What can I do? Love them and appreciate a planet which brought them into existence. Such focus is empowering. This is not an attempt to control eight billion other people; it is accepting the world in which I live and directing my energy in my Universe. When I see how imperfection is necessary for creation and acknowledge my courage in being here, I allow my fear. My knees might still be shaking, but I will dive into the pool and do my best to swim.

Two Points of Consciousness

We are that which chooses and the Universe is that which responds to our choice.

Law of attraction teachings advise against telling the Universe we **need** something (money, for example) as more **needing** is what we'll get. I think such warnings are the reason we fear our energy. They put us smack dab in front of a wall we can't climb. And then we scramble around hoping affirmations will provide a foothold. They won't. Pretense will not help us. You know who feels abundant? Our Light. You know who isn't needy? Our Light.

We are each a package deal – a Story-self and an astonishing Light. Two points of consciousness. If the creative medium had nothing but my human code to read, I'd be in trouble. All manner of resistance would arise and my pool of reality would turn to a raging ocean primed to consume me. Fear would run amok as I'd have no counterpoint focused on what it is I **do** want.

Thank God I am not a single point of consciousness and this little Light of mine, isn't little at all. She is astonishing. I love that descriptor, which means startling in an unexpected way, beyond the realms of plausibility, mind-boggling and inconceivable. Every spiritual teaching I am drawn to presents methods of aligning with our Light. Feel the inner body, observe our thoughts, meditate, practice being mindful, question our beliefs, open our hearts, connect with source, surrender, spend time in nature and my favorite – get a dog.

Ernest Holmes taught *the Universe can only do **for** us, what it can do **through** us.* This stipulation is far less distressing when we know *us* means our Story and our Light. Disconnected emotions are only problematic when we take them too seriously, feed them continuously, and fail to use them as broken ground for growing. Fortunately, tapping into our Light addresses each one of these tendencies.

The Rabbit Hole

Many spiritual paths have taken a club to the Story-self. Christianity claims the natural man is an enemy to God, calls us to repentance, offers an atonement for sins and the blessing of heaven (away from here) is the desired outcome. Eastern religions encourage right action and belief to relieve suffering, attain enlightenment and exit the death/rebirth cycle. Other spiritual teachings describe the ego as dysfunctional, label the mind a psychotic roommate, claim being human is a mistake we've fallen into and encourage us to ditch as much of our story as possible. Even though I prefer less dogmatic teachings, the message I receive repeatedly is my Story is not the villain; it's the objective.

As astonishing as our Light may be, this game is about the story. The one we choose. Our Light isn't pushing us toward a preferred reality - illuminating one pathway while obscuring others. Her goal is not to help us avoid hell or be spared a return visit here. Her intention is not to push enlightenment or help us transcend our ego. I am serious. We show up in a storyline – learn about someone who was saved, awakened out of suffering, paid their karmic debt, or changed the world in a positive way and decide **we want** that experience. The possibility of merging our Story with our Light appeals to us and our Light responds. The expansion was not Her idea – it was our idea. We were not created to do Life's bidding.

Eckhart Tolle suggests instead of *asking what we want from Life*, a more powerful question is to *ask what Life wants from us*. A viable option with meaningful potential. But don't assume it is a universal directive. They don't exist - unless we decide to create a reality where they do. Paradox surrounds us. Things true and false at the same time. It is hard to wrap one's mind around such freedom, to be a God determining the nature of reality. To have such volition.

I do suspect there is a bleed-over effect between our various lives and that our Light is more involved than I'm making Her out to be. She and I may share an agenda. But if all the other me's are doing all the other things, then opportunity costs are of little concern. And every possible path has value. I apologize if these ruminations are giving you a headache. They are giving me a headache and how far down the rabbit hole do I want to go? Far enough to make this point: when we come to know our desire is the hub upon which our story wheel turns, we find empowerment.

Our Own Universe

The idea we each inhabit a Universe all our own is not beyond the scope of possibility. Perhaps the childhood perception of the world revolving around us wasn't such a distortion after all. What are the ramifications here? For starters, it tells me to stop believing anyone else is wrong, for how can they be? They are a God creating in their world, and it doesn't matter what I think about their explorations. It's not my business.

Empowerment does not seek to be THE God, with dominion over others, but A God, who assumes Her rightful position upon the throne of Her own reality. All attempts to usurp power from another's Universe weaken us in our own.

I so yearned for control to give me what I wanted I refused to see how rarely it did. After leaving a religion many of our family are still in, scrambles for control show up regularly. They want to bring us back to the fold and we want them to let it go already. Influence from either side is negligible. We haven't returned and they haven't stopped wanting us to. Each time another jumps into our Universe and tries to take our power, we resent them. Each time we jump into someone else's Universe and try to take their power, they resent us. We leave our own worlds neglected and come back empty-handed. Reality turns into one extended fight (even if its surface appearance is civil), and a life that could please us withers in neglect. No one is there to tend it.

Empowerment is knowing what you want for yourself and keeping your focus there. It is caring for your own garden and remaining in your own castle. When the desire for control tugs at me, coaxing me to leave, I imagine myself descending my throne, lowering the drawbridge, and walking away from my kingdom. Is there freedom in my realm? Appreciation? Acceptance? If I am gone, there is not. All the energy lives in me, so when I depart, the lights shut off behind me.

Stoking the Fires

This analogy works. Are you in your own kingdom or somewhere else? If the answer is somewhere else, turn around and go back. Cross the drawbridge and ascend your throne. Look around and ask yourself, *what's in my kingdom?* and note what you see. Our power lives here. Are we home enough to affect our own world?

Fortunately, I'm not gone all the time. I look around and see appreciation in my kingdom - football games, migrating geese and hot cinnamon cider. Crisp autumn air and red maple leaves in front of the bluest skies. There is connection in my kingdom with family outings and bonus grandkids. Our daughter's new boyfriend has a four-year-old son who couldn't be cuter. The first time we met him, he picked and devoured four tomatoes and a cucumber from our garden. When I offered to help him find strawberries, he said, "No, thank you, I prefer the vegetables!" Last weekend while fishing, he eagerly held a net to secure whatever his dad caught; confidently placed an order for a grilled cheese sandwich and informed us he's getting drums and a guitar for Christmas. There is happiness in my kingdom.

I envision this vast courtyard dotted with magical firepits, each representing an aspect of my empire. Which fires are burning brightly? The fuel is my focus, and no one accesses the woodpile but me. I decide where I look and what I see. Build a bonfire of what you want; stir the coals until they glow hot, and add even more wood. Your attention is an accelerant. Be emboldened as heat radiates in response to you.

It is lamentable to sit around in the cold, wishing Life would warm us when we're in charge of fuel. We can't live empowered until we understand how being a God in our own Universe works. The job is simple - stay in our own business, in our own kingdom, fueling our own fires. What we want exists and is summoned through the essence of its energy.

Road Report: Do you ever find yourself sneaking into your children's kingdom, trying to fuel their fires so they can be happy (and you can be happy)? I do. A straight-up Law of Attraction conundrum. I get their lives are not mine to create, yet their wellbeing is inseparable from my own. There are no parties in a kingdom where your kids are suffering.

What can be done? Look closer at this analogy. Create on your own behalf. Stay in your own realm. You are not choosing for them - you are choosing for you. And a version of everything exists in your Universe. Let the impact of this statement sink in - **a version of everything exists in your Universe.**

This epiphany (the crux of empowerment) is usually a head trip followed by a trip up. Because the first thing we'll go after is control. Knowing there are realities where our children are thriving will push us to reject what is and demand better. I've had some success with this approach (which I'll share later) but not enough to recommend it fully.

Until we can accept what is and what may be (making peace with imperfection), we'll be hauling around buckets of water trying to put out fires we don't want. And resistance is fuel. Go to your woodpile and fill up your cart. Stop first at the fire of allowing and stoke that baby good. Stay there until you are warmed through. Then drop some logs on support. Spark your sense of peace and connection. Add to courage and compassion. Trust your Light and feel Her love for you. Trust your children's Light and feel its love for them. No one is alone here and this fire is worth sitting by.

Make Me a Believer

The Law of Attraction is one way of understanding how the creative medium works. Succinctly, it means that which is like unto itself is drawn. Friend, I assume you already know a lot about this subject. Like me, I imagine you've given it much thought and put it into practice and also like me, achieved mixed results. Doubts crop up. Even though I know I've attracted many things, misgivings arise and I struggle to approach the process fearlessly. The remedy is to strengthen our belief in the Law of Attraction and our confidence in self. For when I purposefully direct my perceptions, reality unfailingly adapts, and certainty I'm the most powerful force in my Universe solidifies for me.

The trick is to put out something BIG. I tend to be lazy and don't give the Law much of significance to reflect. A tepid, half-hearted effort on my part will not pack enough punch to move me into a changed reality. Baby steps aren't going to make me a believer. Move energy in a momentous way and be converted. <u>We influence our own lives,</u> and this lesson needs reinforcing.

Stamp out uncertainty through experimentation. Pinpoint the essence of what you are wanting and hit that BIG. Keep in mind the objective is to up one's belief, not resolve longstanding difficulties. Pick a desire less emotionally weighted and strike with impact.

Presently, we have a daughter looking for housing. Idaho is a hotspot location, and people are moving here from all over the country. Home prices are rising, and rentals in short, expensive supply. Buying a property now seems advisable. But the process hasn't been smooth sailing. We put in an offer on an appealing, older home, only to have the inspector recommend the complete replacement of all electrical and plumbing systems. It's back to the drawing board, and an opportunity to affect my life is right before me. Can I go BIG and find empowerment? The surface request is a home for our daughter, but what is the core request? The underlying nature of what is wanted? *Support. Ease. Appreciation. Wellbeing.*

Let's get this ball rolling and comb through my reality until I find these energies. Until they stand up and stand apart. Until they hold my attention like capital letters. BIG. PROMINENT. PARAMOUNT.

Things always work out –

Our older daughter and her husband recently bought a house in Boise, which is practically a miracle considering their budget and the bench area they wanted to be in. Their English degrees were put to good use, as the letter they wrote led to their not-the-highest offer being accepted. (The seller was a retired librarian.) The inspection was favorable, the appraisal high enough, and unexpected funds came in from both their jobs. A friend from college is going to live with them. A nearby relative has a covered trailer available for their move. The property has a sizeable yard, lots of natural light, and ample storage space. The kitchen boasts a wood-burning stove in front of a brick wall that couldn't be more inviting. Their cat, Archer, is chuffed. Things always work out. *Support. Ease. Appreciation. Wellbeing.*

Unexpected good things happen –

Four gorgeous, free-range turkeys keep escaping their confines and wandering down my street. I'd be challenged to portray how handsome these birds are or how thrilled I am to see them. Even the online updates please me, as my neighbors report recent sightings so the owners can find their fowl and get them home. I know catching and returning these adventurous critters must be a hassle, but I like it when they're on the lam! (It turns out most fowl come and go as they please. Who knew?) Random, perhaps, but such incidents reinforce my belief that unexpected good things happen. *Support. Ease. Appreciation. Wellbeing.*

So much to be thankful for –

Dandelion seeds of blessings have blown across my world. Thomas Edison dahlias splashing huge purple blooms throughout my garden. Influential women's costumes for my tiny granddaughters (Ruth Bader Ginsberg and Amelia Earhart!) Discussions about *The Queen's Gambit*. A biographical book by Mikel Jollet and a renewed love for his music in my life. Thriving nieces and nephews. An uninterrupted night's sleep. A sciatic nerve that has calmed down. Chase Elliot winning a NASCAR championship. Warm weather in November. Posole soup with just the right spiciness. My bounty is endless. *Support. Ease. Appreciation. Wellbeing.*

As I cast about for material that discernably shifts energy for me, I am moved in a BIG way. Life has my back, and I don't need to worry. **Things**

always work out. Unexpected good things happen. There is so much to be thankful for. Having consciously offered up a definitive position for the Law of Attraction to respond to, my job now is to relax into the acceptance of what happens.

Nearly a month has gone by since I hit this BIG. All kinds of house-hunting adventures have ensued. A most disgruntled cat at an open house of *The Short People Place*, gave us this nasty look before retreating into a closet corner. An inebriated schmoozer of a real estate agent at *The Fake Photos House* kept insisting offers were coming in left and right and that a frightening basement - wasn't. We got drawn into a bidding war over a property our daughter had seen, but my husband and I hadn't. We discovered the home was in horrible shape. We satirically named it *The Pool House* (for the collapsed above-ground swimming structure in the backyard), and even though the location was ideal, we backed out of what was likely to be a money pit situation. *The Joanna Gaines House* had the cutest kitchen imaginable but was sadly located on a busy, busy road. A neighbor's massive gray cat greeted us with leg rubs before stepping confidently (and first in line) through the door to see for himself what *The Best Garage House* had to offer.

And then we found *The Grandma House.* While dated, it was super-sound and exceptionally homey. We put in an offer, the acceptance of which was slow in coming, and we feared the property might sell to someone else. Over and over, I ask my Light to help me understand. Again and again, She answers. Empowerment is not the control of conditions but alignment with energy. When we are attached to specifics, we add fear, neediness, and lack to the mix, and outcomes reflect this. A particular home is a condition; support, ease, appreciation, and wellbeing are not.

Assimilate this distinction and your story will shift. Even if a desired yes ends up a disheartening no. Had this opportunity fallen through (it did not), I would have been disappointed but not disempowered.

No God exists who is cryptically granting or denying our requests. No outcome reflects our worthiness, just our humanness, which is fine. Go with the flow and be empowered. Trust no matter how many winding roads we take, the Light is maneuvering on our behalf. We don't have to reach zero fear before the Law of Attraction can reflect welcome things. Never forget our focus and that of our Inner Being are both in play. We aren't alone, and we aren't being asked to quash our humanness.

I was fearful we wouldn't get *The Grandma House*. The move towards empowerment was letting that be okay. I was concerned about my attachment to a particular outcome. The move towards empowerment was allowing this to be. As I consciously aligned with support, ease, appreciation, and wellbeing, reflections of these energies show up everywhere. Empowered, I find myself a believer.

Not a Test

The Law of Attraction asks us to put it to the test. To measure its legitimacy by *focusing deliberately and observing the results*. Doing so convinced me many times over. But eventually, I realized you only keep testing what you doubt and <u>proving grounds invite fear</u>. We put the Universe on trial and make a ruling, but don't let our decision stand. If I know Life has my back, why am I still looking for evidence that maybe it doesn't? Each time I project a pinpoint desire out into the Universe, I set a test in motion. Will Life respond affirmatively? Am I a match to letting this happen? Yes or No.

137

Right or Wrong. Enough or Not Enough. Anxiety sullies what I want to create because proving my worthiness and confirming my take on reality are a dominant part of the mix.

The solution is straightforward: withdraw from a testing paradigm.

What I have to say next supports those who doubt the Law of Attraction. Evidence of our creatorship is inconclusive and it always will be. This is so because the mechanics driving this illusion are exceedingly complex. Reality is not a simple equation where two addends equal a sum. There are more parts in play than we could begin to identify. We are not single-faceted Gods. Our energy will never be one-dimensional (the reason for mixed results), but that is no cause for despair. I made myself a believer, not because I discovered irrefutable proof for my position but because I amassed sufficient evidence to stay this course.

Life is happy to work with our humanness. Let what happens, happen and step out from under the microscope. No evaluation is taking place. We are always enough, even when it could be argued we are doing everything wrong. In the big picture, of course, we can't do experience wrong, but our fear will muck things up. No worries. The human self has been described as the bravest part of the soul, and we've already completed the only task required. Show up. And here we are - mission accomplished.

I want to return to my house-hunting ventures with my daughter and share another story. As we approached a mid-week closing date for *The Grandma House*, I knew it would be beneficial to complete the process sooner. Self-reflection revealed how fear drove me to make nonspecific requests and I decided to be brave. Applying what I've learned, I put a definitive desire out into the Universe. *I would like the signing to be on the 11th and clarified why.* I set a yes/no appeal into motion and then affirmed <u>it was</u>

not a test. I felt no qualms over asking because the situation had nothing to do with my worth or the beneficence of Life. After phoning the bank, our loan officer declined to expedite matters, and that appeared to be that. We accepted the original date and planned accordingly. Then, a last-minute email arrived requesting the document signing be moved to the morning of the 11th. Pleased and appreciative, I noted what was more telling - I felt no relief or validation. There is no stamp of approval in a non-test situation, no roller-coaster of high/low emotions, no holding your breath until the score is posted. Effective creators don't inhabit extremes because they aren't needy. The bliss of alignment is not precarious but sure, as it hinges on nothing that happens here.

Focus on specifics fearlessly by diffusing concern over outcomes. Not getting precisely what we want doesn't expose a lack of worthiness or reveal Life's indifference. It's merely a plot twist in a compelling human story. There are times when I want the least amount of responsibility possible and other times, I want a horse in the race. When I affirm *this is not a test*, I can heartily call for my horse to win and still accept whatever happens.

To call for a win is to make a demand of Life. A process I told you I've had success with but don't fully recommend. The reason being, specifics tend to pull me into control and away from kinder energies. Getting what I want through coercion is not truly getting what I want because fear remains and connection is lacking.

Insight Number One

Manifesting is using deliberate focus to attract or create things we want. Concerned with particulars, it is a spotlight application of empowerment.

Before delving into this topic, however, we must understand the energies we long to live in do not come to us through form. Let's call this truth *Insight Number One* because it paves the way. If such knowledge isn't under our feet at all times, we'll walk where we don't want to go and wonder what happened.

Empowerment is a clear energy. We tend to lose clarity along our path because we're overlooking *Insight Number One*: **form is reflective, not originative.** Results make sense when we get this and make little sense when we don't. I'm reminded of an anecdote told by a wedding officiant who was approached by a young bride. With great relief, she told him in finding her spouse, she'd come to the end of her troubles. He kindly responded she was right, not having the heart to tell her which end.

The primary impediment to a satisfying life is erroneous causation. We suppose particular plotlines in our story will summon the wellbeing we long for, and when they don't, we're left confused. Maybe a different scenario will make us happy, and the chase for improved situations is on. When we don't apply *Insight Number One,* disillusionment inevitably follows.

Look at what you hope to gain and seek it in its formless state. Freedom, connection, and peace are all around us. No unfolding is apart from the truth of who we are and our Light will reveal this. Lack is a misperception alignment corrects. Once we feel the abundance we are, the definitive shape our reality assumes is extraneous. We live content with what arises.

It is not a misstep to focus on specifics, only to believe specifics offer what they don't. A lack of attachment arises of its own accord when we create from a position of already BEING what we desire to express. You're good. I'm good. It can't be otherwise, so let's probe further into our power to craft realities that please us.

Deliberate Focus

It is something to be able to paint a particular picture, or to carve a statue, and so make a few objects beautiful; but it is far more glorious to carve and paint the very atmosphere and medium through which we look. To affect the quality of the day – that is the highest of arts.
~ Henry David Thoreau

I work for rich people whose entitlement can be off the charts. It is fascinating to see up close how excess money is no predictor of wellbeing. Some with wealth are generous, easygoing, and enjoyable to be around, while others are the most miserable, demanding, unpleasant humans one could encounter. When I decided to open my own alterations shop, I aimed to attract pleasing customers. I'd sit in the sunshine, enjoy a snack, and purposefully appreciate all the generous, interesting people I've been privileged to know. It worked like a charm. A screaming lady appeared one morning, pounding on my door and window. When I told her I wasn't yet open but was glad to help her with whatever she needed, she went silent and walked away. Another time, a furious person phoned who couldn't find my shop (located on the corner of main street as you entered town) and even though I confirmed my address with directions, they never showed up.

A woman reached out wanting some items altered to better fit her petite size. She immediately told me about unsatisfactory work others had done for her and asked if I was any good at what I do. It was not an auspicious beginning. Knowing there might be complications, I deliberately looked for things to like about her while being confident in my mad sewing skills. The transaction went fine. She was pleased with my work and life went on.

Fast forward a year. After months of living abroad, she'd returned to Idaho and brought in a pile of complicated alterations she insisted be completed perfectly and immediately. To shorten a long, unpleasant story, she was displeased with a dress she'd asked me to make into a blouse, and I found myself writing her a check for $300. The dress was given to her by a friend who was clearing closet space, but she estimated this amount to be its value. I think I was as irritated by her sharing this information as I was about having to pay her!

Livid when I declined to do any more work for her, she demanded another sewer recommendation. Seriously? I gave her a contact number so she'd leave and then immediately called my seamstress friend with a heads-up. My now-former customer was mad. I was mad and the whole situation was regrettable. There were layers of lessons here when it comes to empowerment. Unlike our first encounter, I had not directed my focus toward appreciation. I was feeling overwhelmed with my workload and her attitude annoyed me. Resistant to doing the work she'd brought in, the energy in place brought about a negative outcome. In no way was I a victim here. I'm not suggesting I caused her to be difficult, but I joined her in a place of things not going well. There were two empowered choices before me, and I didn't make either of them. I could have shifted my energy to affect the unfolding or set a boundary and declined to do the work. No one forces our hand and we are not at the mercy of a world apart from us.

There are times when this truth is a bitter pill to swallow. We want someone to blame, and we don't want that person to be us. But the fact I chose poorly is of far less import than the fact I was the one choosing. Our focus influences outcomes and we will never know our power until we can connect those dots. It is helpful to activate worthiness and empowerment together. If I berate myself for a slip up, I make a bad situation worse. If I feel worthy while acknowledging my part in what happened, I'm encouraged. My worth and my customer's worth exist apart from this situation. Our shortcomings are irrelevant in the vast, overwhelming truth of who we are. I can value another person and choose not to work with them at the same time.

We spin our stories and decide what they mean. This incident was the impetus I needed to start referring jobs out and saying no to requests I didn't want to do. I have plenty of sportswear to alter and don't care to work on designer clothing. It's my good fortune to have a friend who was a fashion designer in Hollywood who does. She sends zippers to me, and I send beaded dresses to her. I don't want all the business in town. I want a manageable number of projects where I do excellent work for pleasant people who pay me well. Clear intentions are empowering and deliberate focus brings those intentions to the forefront.

Negative Wanting

When my husband's grandfather passed away, we were given this awesome 1970 ford truck. For twenty-five years, it was a great vehicle for yard work and dump runs. Getting ten miles to the gallon, though, meant it wasn't great for travel, so we decided to buy a Tundra. A family member wanted the classic Ford but never came to get it. An eyesore in the front yard, strangers would stop by our house wanting to buy and restore it, but we were in this awkward position of holding it for someone who wasn't making its retrieval a priority. (Boundary issues – I know.) Then, a tree branch broke. The damage was slight but provided a push for the truck's removal. I expected to feel better once it was gone, but I didn't. The situation held energies of irritation (that it sat there so long) and resentment/guilt (over judgments we didn't take better care of it), and those remained - verifying the adage wherever you go, there you are.

There is a kind of manifesting I call <u>negative wanting</u>, which is a desire to remove a condition from our life. Wanting to be rid of something is a dicey undertaking as it tends to advance resistance and keep us stuck. Even if the condition changes, the unsettled energy remains.

We live on the boundary of our city limit where it is against the rules to have livestock. The neighbors behind us are in the country and we enjoy their sheep who graze in the fields nearby. The neighbors to the side of us are also in town and recently acquired two calves and a goat. They are penned right next to the swing, where I drink my morning coffee and enjoy the mountain views. The cows are cute but attract black flies. The goat is a new arrival, and (fingers crossed) we hope she'll stop her loud bawling once she gets used to her new home. We could complain, but we like our neighbors. They've been so generous in keeping a mature tree that is on their property but canopies our home, providing shade and a branch for a swinging bench we built.

This is an on-target example of negative wanting. We want the mini-farm to go away. We want to avoid contention with our neighbors. But as anyone with a basic understanding of the Law of Attraction knows, what you resist persists. The creative medium forming reality registers focus – Life follows attention – so we get more of what we fixate upon. Negative wanting may change circumstances but is unlikely to resolve the discord attached to an unwelcome reality. How do we maneuver such situations? Abraham teaches when you know what you don't want, you also know what you do. But if I'm sitting in my backyard and catch a whiff of cow manure, negative wanting is part of that equation.

Neutrality is often the best I can shoot for, and acceptance will take me there. Solve a problem in short order by allowing what is to be. Of course, I wish the only scent in the air was that of flowers and cut grass, but that isn't my current reality, and this problem will be as big as I decide it is. It's **mind over matter**, for *the less I mind, the less it matters.* I'm not espousing some flim-flam claim I now like flies and enjoy the goat's screaming. I'm consenting to what I don't want with less protest. Smaller fight.

The animals were gone as suddenly as they arrived. Our neighbor's two-week plan was to move them out to the country with relatives, but it took three months instead. In the meantime, I drank my morning coffee on the other side of our yard. After a few days, the goat quieted down and would approach our fence to stamp her foot at my dog, which made me smile. The pens are still up and come Spring, the mini-farm may return. Empowerment is not a demand that transforms everything to our liking; it is a conscious shift in focus to lessen entitlement and expand peace.

White Peaches

Standing in my garden one morning, I found myself looking at our nectarine tree. It's had a rough life. We moved it once and shortly after it was smashed to the ground by a falling pallet. (Growing strawberries vertically was a bust.) I let some sucker branches grow, hoping to save the little tree. Seasons passed and it rallied, producing nectarines on one side and tiny peaches on the other. We have another tree which yields large, delectable fruit, so I'd given little attention to the small ones and usually left them for the squirrels.

We ought to plant another peach tree, I thought, *one with white peaches as they taste so good.* Considering possible sites, I distractedly picked a few tiny peaches for a snack and headed inside. As I peeled and sliced the little fruits, I was taken by surprise to see the flesh was white. Wow - nothing like a five-minute time-lapse between asking and receiving! What was it about this wanting that led to such a speedy resolution?

It was a reasonably strong desire and one I had complete confidence could happen, not in minutes, but certainly within a couple of years. I jumped straight from yearning to the sweet spot of *you will be mine.* No hurdles stood between us. No fear, no attachment, no conflict, no doubts, no unpleasant reality to correct. Logic would argue this was nothing but a fortunate coincidence, which may be the case. In the absence of interference, however, unlikely circumstances seem more the rule than exception for me.

Again - *We are that which chooses, and the Universe is that which responds to our choice.* The commonness of getting stuck in the asking phase reveals not a lack of power but the rarity of unambiguous requests. We encumber movement through our own complexity. Much of what I want is nothing like white peaches, which is as it should be. Empowerment expands when I acknowledge profound manifestations (like this one) that show up in remarkable ways when no internal contradictions convolute the process.

Pushmi-pullyu

In the children's book *Doctor Doolittle*, a fictional, llama-like character had two heads, one on each side of his body. Called a pushmi-pullyu, its conflicted nature brings to mind a common difficulty in manifesting - opposing desires.

A friend of mine had been single for a long time. She wanted to date but was hesitant to enter a new relationship. She loved freedom and did not want to be controlled. And as that had been her experience before, she was afraid to repeat it. Two obvious heads here. Human stories are full of such dilemmas.

When something we want is slow to arrive (or doesn't arrive at all,) a pushing/pulling dynamic is usually in play. Impulses to go left and right at the same time move us nowhere. Unconscious thoughts could be running in the background (we don't know we fear losing our freedom, for example,) but I've never found this issue to be that complicated. If a desire isn't showing up, answering the simple question of *why wouldn't I want this?* solves what isn't much of a mystery.

The most pertinent pushmi-pullyu in my story would be finishing this book. I want to do it and don't want to do it at the same time. Which would explain the snail's pace at which it's proceeded. I don't even need to ask *why wouldn't I want this?* to reveal the conflicts. It's a no-brainer.

Hurdles: Writing a book is hard. Colossally hard. It's too much. The magnitude overwhelms me, and I struggle to focus small. Getting started is miserable, so I find reasons to avoid writing at all. (We're going camping tomorrow and I should prepare this morning while the garage is cool.)

Doubts: I have confidence in my ability to teach but less in my ability to write. I've never wanted to be a writer. Plus, I'm not an enlightened being, and only enlightened beings should share their journeys.

Downsides: People may think these ideas are nonsense. I prefer living under the radar, and this kind of work is too exposing. It's time that could be spent gardening or bird watching or walking in the desert or napping or reading a book someone else wrote.

Fear of Change: Finishing will bring unknown changes. Things are pleasing right now, so why risk it?

Identity: I need to do this to be of value in the world. I need to do this because my husband has supported me on this path, and if I don't finish it, I will let him down. I need to do this, or I will let myself down.

It's pretty obvious why it's taking so long to let this happen. I'm being pulled in too many directions. The expansive energy of *nothing to prove, everything to explore* is being dominated by the confining energy of *something to prove, dangerous, and difficult to explore.*

As I wrapped up my daily writing (completing what you just read) and went about my business, a depressed mood fell over me. Out of sorts, I moped around, wondering what I'd done to focus my way into this discouraged feeling. At first, I suspected I'd ingested some political poison, then realized in sharing my struggles, I'd gone back into a pushmi-pullyu dynamic and was feeling the worst part of it all over again. A part I've moved beyond. Like visiting a childhood home or attending a class reunion, I'd returned to an emotional place I no longer inhabit and things were off.

A transformation in my energy had occurred but I wasn't cognitive of the tempering. My conflicts over finishing *Thoughts That Move Energy* had shifted by first validating the interference and then going beyond it.

Hurdles: Writing a book is hard, but I can do hard things. Baby steps are all that is being asked of me, and those are manageable. One sentence, one paragraph, one-half page most days. As Tolkien said, *little by little one travels far.*

Doubts: I am a better teacher than a writer, and that's okay. A highly competent source is assisting me, which is a good thing. All I need do is find thoughts that move energy for me and share those thoughts with MY friends - no one else. And my friends are exceptionally kind, so that's good too. My heart's desire is to teach and the medium for that is writing. If enlightened people were the only ones to share their journeys, a staggering amount of beauty would go unexpressed in this world.

Downsides: I'm going to let the upsides of this undertaking matter more. Every time I find a thought that moves energy, my life improves. Every time I connect with my Light to create what is meaningful to me, the mystery deepens. Every time I stretch myself in a world with limits from a foundation without limits, I expand possibility here.

Fear of Change: Why not embrace the freedom of letting whatever happens happen? What is there to lose, really? If dahlias don't bloom, there are always ranunculus! This adventure is mine. It's going to unfold in a million ways, and there will be love and fear in all of them. Fear is not a deal-breaker, but a deal-enabler and I choose to let that be.

Identity: Nothing about this desire has anything to do with the inherent value of my story. It doesn't. When I let this knowing arise, love embraces me. We are not imposters in a game we've snuck into. We needn't worry we'll be found out. The Animating Force expresses Life through us and what is happening here is unparalleled. Meaning absolutely everything and utterly nothing at the same time, empowerment drives it all, for *we have nothing to prove and everything to explore* in our stories.

If you only shift one conflict, let it be identity. Nothing will walk you in circles quicker than tying your worth to something you accomplish. The idea I would let myself down if I didn't finish this book is the thought that was killing me. It hurt so much and was the greatest untruth I chose to believe. My story wasn't capable of righting this wrong, but my Light was. Turn in that direction when you fear measuring up. Let your Light show you how impossible that is. Detrimental assumptions will shift without villainizing our human perceptions.

Our pushmi-pullyus may have fifty heads, and every one of them is welcome. Give them respect while affirming those which reflect our highest truths. Make peace with contradictions and let our Light help us bridle the heads we want to lead.

As You Wish

The creative medium is not a decision-maker but a decision-carry-outer. Could it speak, its only words would be *As You Wish*. Mirroring our attention, it confirms what we choose to believe. We spend time in nature and think *This is heavenly*! and the medium responds with *It really is, isn't it? Smell these pine trees, aren't they divine?* We come across a story and exclaim, *Man, that is wild!* and the medium replies *Isn't that the truth? Check out this tale over here!* We complain *Life is just one damn thing after another* and the medium follows up with *Damn straight it is! Here comes another problem now.*

At times I've doubted how accurate this hypothesis (that we create our own reality) is because events I didn't expect or focus upon occurred. But ask yourself these questions: Do I believe the unexpected can happen? That I can get hurt or sick here? That vulnerability is part and parcel of human life? The sobering fact is not a single thing has happened in my reality that I didn't believe could happen. Take this information and do with it what you will. I choose to cut myself slack for being human in a human place and make no attempt to micromanage my beliefs. I tried that and it made me miserable.

We are Gods creating here. But could we fully comprehend this truth, it's likely the illusion would spit us out. We can't experience this fantasy as real unless a significant part of us believes it is. <u>Infallibly creating a paradise for ourselves would be game over.</u>

Game on. It's middle ground I'm after. To maintain enough of the illusion to be here but not so much I'm tortured by it. Empowered to affect my life, without erasing all contrast. Frankly, I've never felt the slightest danger of dissolving the illusion (even in moments of great connection.) This world has taken me in, as intended.

But here is a hot tip coming straight from my Light: <u>All that is necessary to change a belief is to hold the desire to believe something else.</u> That's it. Think themes here. If I tell the creative medium I **want** to believe I am supported, evidence of support will begin showing up. If I desire to believe life is worth living, confirmation is on its way. If I say I **want** to believe there is cause for hope, reasons to be hopeful will make my radar.

Road Report: As I sit here this morning, the United States is in the middle of a pandemic, a week away from a presidential election, and reality is striking me as one enormous shitshow. (I get this precarious point in time will resolve and you, my friend, have already lived through what happens.) But the sensation of being out on a limb and not knowing if, or when, or how the branch might break, shows up in repeatedly in our timelines. Looking at an unsettled present won't yield me a crystal ball answer but can help me be more empowered in my approach.

Right now, I feel like I am constantly on guard to avoid being trampled by collective anxiety. I'm surrounded by people who think the virus is a hoax and Donald Trump is a righteous dude. What utterly insane story have I fallen into? Even Halloween has turned political. In my tiny community, a fight broke out online. The consensus from opposing sides seems to be if you aren't handing out candy, you're a patsy controlled by fear and if you are handing out candy, you're willing to let people die rather than be inconvenienced. Ludicrous. Byron Katie would describe this as God's business, not mine, and I concur. My business is my reality, and such animosity is not what I want!

C. S. Lewis said our neighbor is the holiest object presented to our senses. Every human I encounter is God standing right in front of me. The Divine presenting itself in form. The Light hanging out with me. Love looking me in the eye. Could there be a more incredible treasure in my life?

But social media puts up this barrier between us and others. The most fundamental aspect of our beings – the mystery we live in and emanate from – is concealed. Too little information makes its way through, and the connection that would heal us is truncated. Our worst egoic intentions tend to surface when our positions feel threatened, and we don't truly see each other. Our responses are harsh and cutting, whether we post those responses or not. Nothing is more painful than living outside the energy of connection.

I **want** to believe the world holds worthy people, that love is finding a way here, that every setback is progress in disguise. When I project this desire out into the cosmos, my reaction turns from a negative (oh, my God – people are unbelievable!) to a positive (oh, my God – people are incredible!) That so many of us are afraid is irrelevant. The Animating Force sourcing all Life is the consequential fact here.

Stop Equivocating

Everything changes when you start to emit your own frequency rather than absorbing the frequencies around you, when you start imprinting your intent upon the Universe rather than receiving an imprint from existence.
~ Barbara Marciniak

Friend, I would like us to ignite the energy of empowerment together. To feel what it is to send a beacon of desire out into the world holding nothing back. To express with absolute certainty what it is we want. No qualifiers. No settling. No ambiguity. No doubts. No steering ourself toward what seems appropriate or attainable.

Set fear aside and stop negotiating. We don't need protection from disappointment. Wanting without need <u>is</u> the end game. The satisfying full expression of our own power. It doesn't matter if we get what we want – it matters if we let ourselves want what we want. Ask yourself, am I equivocating? Waffling because I imagine I am stepping out of line? Forgetting my place? Setting myself up for a fall?

There can be no fall, so let's blow up the damn box already! The one holding us in check, telling us where we can and can't go, limiting our growth and keeping us small. Light the match and toss it. I am an astonishing Light in need of nothing, creating in a world that belongs to me. It is MY Universe, so let me be clear.

I want to see an Andean Condor fly and be overwhelmed by magic. Literally brought to my knees by the wonder of this incomparably beautiful planet. I want my son to call me with news their game is making enough money for him and his wife to start their own company and be overcome by support. To hear excitement in his voice and know beyond doubt opportunities exist here. I want a revolution in my lifetime – an energetic one where exploitive systems crumble and build into better – so much better. A world where connection means no one has to suffer or die for this to happen and no ongoing battle is necessary to keep it in place.

What I feel when I clarify my own desire is power. There is no wishy/washy uncertainty here. I may very well find myself living in and learning to accept realities that are not my first choices but that won't be because I'm unclear as to what my first choices are. The energy of empowerment is not about rising to assert our will but refusing to shy away from our own truths. We came here to express the astonishing Light of our Being as a Story; to be the critical piece in this particular human game; to explore time and space in a Universe all our own and love ourselves along this journey.

Conclusion

Friends, as I bring this book to a close, I want you to know how much you mean to me and how grateful I am for your contribution here. Every morning, I communicate with my Light and Her primary encouragement is to write for the right people. That's you. We are friends on the road and even though the constraints of being a Story-self means we're unlikely to meet here, we are known to each other in the Light.

My husband asked if I planned to build a website for my book, with all the social media trappings and I answered that I had no intention of doing any of those things. Selling myself as a product feels off and would consume time better spent finishing my second book - *More Thoughts that Move Energy.* I'm thrilled to continue writing for you each morning and delve into the life-changing energies of freedom, worthiness, enthusiasm, ease, and connection.

But then a message came through, reminding me that I am free to play this game any way I want. A website could be less about branding and more about coming together as the kith and kin we are. I've secured the domain name (thoughtsthatmoveenergy.com) and the idea of an online gathering place where we share our stories, insights, and experiences with energy (and of course, photos of our dogs!) is sparking my imagination. This potential has connection written all over it and friend, if you feel so inclined, I'd love for you to add your vision to this undertaking as well.

About the author

Julie Merrick is currently inhabiting an exceptionally supportive and engaging reality. She and her husband, Steve, are adjusting to retirement. They've yet to move from their small Idaho town and find themselves battling a vole infestation in a valiant attempt to save their garden. Their chill cat Morty is doing well but anxious for them to pull the trigger and bring home a corgi (a little girl they've decided to name Ivy). The Swainson's hawks have returned from Argentina but there is no evidence of any babies this year.

Julie has learned more about self-publishing in the last few months than she ever wanted to know but now a completed book is on her bucketed list, so she doesn't mind. She continues to reach for a smaller fight, allowing the political craziness that seems determined to last forever. Over and over, she returns to Her Kingdom and stokes the fires of her choosing. Present enough to feel good while enjoying the popcorn and the animals. After watching the World Cup last year, soccer has been added to her pile of good things and WHO she is becoming in loving herself is a journey she's glad to be taking.

Printed in Dunstable, United Kingdom